JOHN I

ONE MILE AT A TIME

THE JOURNEY TOWARD AN UNBREAKABLE BOND WITH MY AUTISTIC SON

outskirts
press

*Dedicated to three special people in my life:
My wife, Lisa, without whom I would be lost
and who has worked tirelessly behind the
scenes to make our family clock tick.
My daughter, Mya, who lives an atypical life as
a sibling of a brother with special needs. You set
a perfect example that all should follow
My son, Cameron, my best friend and someone
who has inspired me far beyond words can
describe and made me a better person.*

Table of Contents

Foreword

I wrote this story in the hopes that it might help someone out there who, like I struggled, is struggling to come to grips with the fact that their son or daughter has autism or is special needs. It took me a long time to find the words to write, mostly because it required complete transparency into our world, into my mind, and into the mistakes made during a time of desperation.

To say this journey has been a rollercoaster is an understatement. Truth be told, some of the biggest transitions we have to face are still in front of us. As I write this book we are in the planning phases for Cameron's after-high-school plan as we transition from having a child with autism in school to having a dependent adult with autism under our roof. I thought figuring out how to have a child with autism was a maze. Having an adult with autism is certainly a scary place as we traverse into paths unknown. However, we will tackle this phase with the lessons learned over the last fourteen years since diagnosis: Seek input from those who have been there, and read, research, and explore. Most of all we will tackle it head on and with all we have in us.

When it comes to raising a child with autism, perhaps one of the most important life lessons I ever learned came in ten written words: "Somewhere out there, someone is dreaming to live your life." I didn't stumble upon those words until a few years ago, but I thought it an important way to start this book. Early on I was way too caught up in what I didn't have, what I wouldn't be able to do with my son, and that life was unfair, etc., to realize that it was more important to plug in and find a way. The easy way out was rationalizing my woe-is-me attitude as justified.

In no way am I saying it was easy. Even today there are times of extreme frustration and times when patience is as thin as the paper this book is printed on. Outwardly I am sure it looks like that. By design we seek to protect our kiddos from outside perception, and social media makes it easy to paint a rosier-than-reality picture. All my Facebook posts focus on the positives of Cam's life and what he has accomplished. I just can't stand for someone to think ill of him, so I am very careful of how I paint the canvas of our day-to-day life.

The fundamental difference in today's moments of frustrations when we are faced with a setback is the bulldog mentality both Lisa and I have developed over the years. They (I'm not sure who "they" are) say a bulldog's snout is designed to both hold on to whatever it is holding on to and breathe at the same time, so as not to grow weary and have to let go.

In many ways this is the perfect description of raising a child with special needs. It is easy to grow weary when fighting for your children. It takes a willing and relentless effort to get the most for them and out of them. Tackling state programming, tackling school systems, standing firm in the face of public judgment, fighting dismissal from family members toward your child, wondering when your next date or "time-out" might be … it all takes its toll. It takes a bulldog mentality to face it all, and it's much easier to tackle with a partner.

My hats off to any single parents out there. We have encountered several in our time raising Cameron. Each time I wonder how in the world they manage. I cannot imagine trying to navigate these waters without Lisa. She is the backbone of our family. Her strength, patience, and love are examples I strive to show daily. She has a resilience that is second to none, and I would most certainly be lost without her.

The tragedy of special-needs parenting is the likelihood of divorce. Depending on where you read the stats, it is two to three times more likely in a marriage impacted with special needs than one that isn't. Ours almost went that route, and I am *so* glad it did not.

Finding Our Feet

Watching Cameron now often takes me back to when he was a young child newly diagnosed with autism, something that thrust all of us headfirst into a world we knew nothing about that would become our new "normal" way of living, though we had no idea at the time.

I suspect it's a familiar story for a lot of us on the surface. You have a child that, at around the age of one and a half to two and a half years old, things just don't feel right. At first you hide your suspicions. You don't talk about them in public, and perhaps as in our case, the husband and wife don't even talk about their suspicions to each other, as if it won't happen if you don't talk about it. Folks are always willing to help you further your denial by relying on old adages. For us it was mostly "Boys always develop slower than girls" or "Don't compare your two kids; they are always on their own timetables," or my personal favorite, "He doesn't need to talk; he's got an older sister talking for him." We bought into it, regardless of the inner suspicion we both had.

As I reflect on the last eighteen years, I often shake my head wondering how we are even still together as a family. Although I am not sure how true to life our story is for others, it is one that can best be described as a rollercoaster that was absolutely centered on my inability, for several years, to come to grips with the fact that I had a child with significant developmental delays, a child with very high needs, a child with autism. My actions reflect those of someone completely self-centered and searching for anything other than the reality of the situation I was in.

Both of our kids were 'surprises'. Lisa and I married young in 1998. We were high school sweethearts and had been together since 1994, aside from some brief breakups. In late fall of 1999, we found out that Lisa was pregnant, and in June 2000, our daughter, Mya, was born. Mya was an absolute angel. Everything was easy with her. She was easily entertained, became an overnight sleeper quickly, and was in general a happy baby who loved to be held and played with. The joy and pride of being a first-time dad is something that is impossible to explain.

Mya was born at a time that I was beginning to find my feet as a responsible man of the house. In many ways she was the catalyst that set my delayed-onset maturity in motion. There is nothing like the tiny hands of a newborn to help you realize that life isn't all about you anymore. It was important to both Lisa and me that Lisa be able to stay home with Mya. We just didn't like the thought of daycare, so we made the necessary changes to make it possible for Lisa to stay at home. The income-and-expense structure we had made, however, became a bit of challenge.

I began to look for ways to make ends meet in a more fulfilling way. Lisa was from Corpus Christi, and much of her family still lived there. I began perusing the job market in that area in the hopes that I could find something that offered more than I could find in our small hometown of Mountain Home, Arkansas. It didn't take long for me to find something down there. Off we went, packing up what little we owned in a moving truck and departing for Corpus Christi with plans to stay with Lisa's family on a very short-term basis while looking for an apartment. Although I had thoroughly researched the job market, I had fallen short in my research of the housing market (in my defense I was only 21 years old at the time). It didn't take long to figure out that I made more money, but the cost of living was substantially higher, though we were determined to get a place of our own. Co-dwelling with another family isn't desirable, and adults should live on their own; at least that was our mindset. Pretty soon we found a small apartment that suited our needs, and we moved in.

We were quickly stretched financially. As we evaluated the situation, our desires remained the same—for Lisa to be able to stay at home with Mya. It meant I had to find one more job than I already had.

Hard work had never been a problem for me. I grew up working on a farm with one of my friends, which meant summer breaks were pretty much sunup to sundown in the fields picking watermelon and cantaloupe or delivering them to local grocers. From there I started working with my stepdad and grandpa in their produce business, which was pretty much a sunup to sundown job as well, so working my day job and then delivering pizzas four nights a week wasn't that big of a deal. I liked delivering pizzas. The job was not physically demanding, although there were some neighborhoods that made this rural-grown boy more than a bit uncomfortable. The weekends offered the best money, as tips would come in more readily. It meant investing an additional twenty to twenty-two hours a week in work complemented with tips provided what I needed to provide for the family. We were beginning to settle into life down in Corpus Christi as a family of three. Little did we know there was a huge change on the horizon that would alter our course significantly.

A Family of Four

The year 2001 will go down as the one that changed everything. I remember it quite clearly, that March day Lisa mentioned she thought she might be pregnant, as there were obvious signs that only a woman would be tuned into. It was something that was neither planned nor desired. It's not that we were against having kids, but the thought of having another baby scared us both.

It was challenging enough to be in this new place, though we did have family in the area, but adding another baby to the mix would double down on the challenges and add to the complexities of the household, as baby Mya was only seven months old. I'll never forget the look on Lisa's face as she came out of the bathroom with the pregnancy test. It was positive, and she was crying. Through tears of fear and worry, we discovered we were having baby number two.

The news of being pregnant again was tough to swallow, and we were in a state of shock and confusion. It slowly became the new reality, and we began to accept the fact that in a few months we would be a family of four. Thankfully my primary job included some excellent insurance, and the prenatal and delivery was paid for with a very small deductible. Although news of being pregnant came as quite a bit of shock and did not line up with where we thought we were headed, we met all the milestones with the joy any parent-to-be would have. We were as enthusiastic about hearing the heartbeat and getting those first few ultrasounds as we had been during Lisa's pregnancy with Mya. The day of the gender reveal, which, might I add, wasn't a thing in those days and was only an ultrasound, brought news that we would soon welcome a baby boy into the world.

I'll admit that the thought of having a son was both exciting and a little scary for me. You know how boys look up to their fathers. Deep inside I wondered if I had what it took to be a good dad. At the same time, I looked forward to football, hunting, fishing, talking about trucks, growing beards, and doing all sorts of other "man stuff" with my little dude. Little did I know I would be tested in ways I could have never predicted.

As is likely common in new marriages, communication wasn't exactly a strong point between Lisa and me. It didn't help that life was filled with chaos of two jobs and settling into a new apartment. Heck, we were still figuring out how to be married, had one baby already, and had another on the way. We were going to have two kids before we were twenty-two. At the same time, we were still trying to establish ourselves in a new and very big city. I was definitely missing home, though I wasn't sure whether it was a product of being young or perhaps just finding out that we were about to welcome a new baby boy into the fold. For several months I kept that feeling to myself. I just couldn't bring myself to tell Lisa that I wanted to move back home. What I didn't know was that she felt the same way and didn't want to tell me. Thankfully one night over dinner I summoned the courage to tell her, only to find out that she felt the same. How relieving that was! Neither one of us were happy living in Corpus Christi; it just didn't feel like home. Of course, moving back home offered its own unique challenges, as smaller communities offered fewer employment opportunities. But we were both aligned with the move being the right direction.

I reached out to friends and family immediately. My focus was securing employment that would keep our family situation the same and allow Lisa to be home with Mya and not stress about having to work.

Moving Back Home

Life is funny, and seemingly insignificant things that happen in the moment have huge implications somewhere down the road, from the things one does to the people one meets. In reflection I have come across many people I owe immensely for their kind deeds toward me. Cameron Davis is one of those people for sure.

Cameron Davis and I met during the days that I worked for my grandpa. The largest volume fruit stand we ran was in front of a Walmart, which was not a supercenter. Cameron would come down on Saturday afternoons and buy tomatoes and the occasional watermelon, which is where I got to know him. There had long been rumor of a supercenter on the books for Mountain Home, and I'd always make the casual remark that if they ever get it ironed out with the city that I'd love to be a Produce manager for him. His reply was always the same and with the same smile, "Come see me when you see we are breaking ground." As luck would have it, Mountain Home and Walmart had finally found common ground and the plans for a supercenter to open in February 2002 was on the books.

When Lisa and I finalized our decision to move back to Mountain Home, he was the first person I reached out to for career advice. He put me in touch with his district manager, and after a quick trip back home to interview, I had secured a great position as a manager trainee, a position that offered more money than I was making, and most importantly, the opportunity to get back home. In late May 2001 we were headed back to where we belonged, home, and about to start on a journey that was as full of twists, turns, ups, and downs as a high-thrills rollercoaster.

On October 26 2001, we welcomed our new boy into the world. We had decided several months earlier that his name would be Cameron. Yeah, yeah, I know, go ahead and accuse me of being a brownnoser. Believe me, I certainly took my share of ribbing from my fellow assistant managers for naming my son after our boss. However, the decision had been made long before Cam was born. It was something my wife decided on as we were in the transition to move back home. Many of our conversations around the new employment opportunity would start with, "I talked to Cameron today and…" or "Did Cameron call today?" In our quest to find a way home in 2001 the name *Cameron* became a household name. When we actually got to the point of the pregnancy where we were deciding names, the conversation lasted about three and a half minutes.

The challenges of having two babies sixteen months apart were obvious from day one. Lisa's parents had been watching Mya while Lisa was in labor and for the eventual C-section. Mya was excited to meet her baby brother, until the moment she walked into the hospital room and saw Lisa holding

Cameron in the hospital bed. Like a light switch, Mya went from smiling to crying. She was not sure how to take the arrival of this new kid. Thankfully that phase passed rather quickly, and by the end of the first day she was completely accepting of her brother.

That was that; we were the proud parents of two kids, except we had no clue to the challenges that lay ahead.

Suspicion, Denial, Acceptance

Cameron was different, and it was obvious to me from day one. I sensed it in the hospital during the times we spent with him. Lisa was in the hospital for a couple of days, and we had Cameron with us as often as possible. His behavior and his comfortableness with being held or fed was very different from what I had experienced with Mya.

I had prepared myself for that possibility to the best of my ability, because throughout the pregnancy people cautioned us that babies are often complete opposites of each other. I rationalized it by reminding myself that Mya was a seventeen-month-old, and I quite possibly could be contrasting the two. In the early days I kept my doubts and suspicions to myself and shoved them in the deepest, darkest places of my mind.

Cameron's first noticeable signs included severe delay and difficulty grasping what should be seemingly easy things. As a baby he was unable to consume more than a quarter of his bottle at a time, as he couldn't grasp the concept of bottle-feeding and was taking in way too much air. Our doctor thought he may have some type of blockage in his esophagus and wanted to do an upper GI series. I still shutter when I think of that experience and watching Cam go through the procedure. He was uncomfortable throughout the procedure and it was incredibly difficult to get the imaging needed. The results from it came back normal, and it was determined that he simply wasn't swallowing appropriately. He would get full, mostly of air, and stop eating, and then he would want to eat forty-five minutes to an hour later, in a continuous cycle twenty-four hours a day.

When I say we looked *everywhere* for a solution, I mean it quite literally. I cannot tell you how many different combinations of bottles and nipples we went through, trying to find the right one. Keep in mind, Cameron was born in 2001, so we did not have the vastness of the web that we have today. Lisa and I would have loved to have read an online forum discussion like what is available today. We turned over every rock we found, trying to find something that would work for him, but to no avail.

When I reflect on Cameron's early childhood, the first year and a half was the most challenging time of his life. I describe it best by simply saying that if he wasn't eating, sleeping, or rocking in his chair, he was crying, and I mean it quite literally. We chalked it up as a colicky baby in the early days, but there seemed to be something more at the root of the issue.

Cameron always seemed to be uncomfortable, and nothing soothed him. There was no consoling or comforting him. His two favorite things were to be wrapped tightly in a blanket and to be in his rocker. Of course, there is a parental guilt side of the latter. We certainly had no desire to simply leave Cameron in a rocker all day, yet trying to do things with him that we did with his older sister was a near impossibility, as it would lead to crying. It's hard to look back on that time knowing now what I didn't know then. I cannot begin to imagine the simple things we could have tried, as he was most likely experiencing significant sensory issues we could have intervened with. I don't know if there were foundational resources available at the time, because I was more interested in being angry about it than trying to make it better.

As you might imagine, frustration ran high in the Leachman household daily. Thank God for the loving patience of Lisa in those days. I was struggling to accept Cameron, because of the extreme challenge he presented. Slowly I withdrew from attempting to make it better. I quietly slipped to a place where blame and disdain were common feelings toward my own son. Each moment of frustration seemed to be a brick in a wall I was building between Cameron and me. Those early years of raising Cameron were so vastly different from just a couple years earlier with Mya. I was 100 percent engaged with Mya and approached it with a daddy's pride and with love. While I would help out with changing and feeding Cam, I dreaded doing so and approached it reluctantly as a chore.

Lisa and I rarely discussed the emerging concerns about Cameron's behavior. She and I were growing apart, though I didn't see it at the time. Of course, it makes sense such would be the case. We weren't talking; we weren't leaning on each other in one of our most challenging times as a young couple. She was trying to keep everything together and provide care, love, and attention to both of our kids, while I was becoming increasingly disconnected from Cameron as his challenges continued to appear. I cannot say for sure what Lisa felt or the concerns she had, because I was much too centered on my own frustrations.

Autism?

I was the first to utter the word *autism*. There were many things that made me believe that Cameron might be showing signs of autism. I was never one to go down the path of denial, perhaps in large part because of my disconnectedness from Cameron from a dad-son point of view. I believe denial is common with many people, and I include Lisa, as she would agree, because of their care, love, and concern for their child. The very thought that something might be wrong with your child is tough to come to grips with.

My disconnectedness and indifference toward Cameron made enabled a more pragmatic approach from me. As sad as it is, the feelings of love, care, and concern were absent in me, so it was easy for me to point a finger and have the courage to face reality.

In addition to Cameron's significant delays, sleepless nights, and emerging signs of sensory sensitivity, he had also started banging his head against the wall or door when he got frustrated. As Lisa and I were discussing this behavior one night with my mom, I said for the first time that I thought Cameron might be autistic. I was very quickly chastised by both Lisa and my mom for saying such a thing. The main objection to my belief was the lack of regression in Cameron. Most diagnoses of autism at the time were precipitated from concern of a normally developing child and subsequent regression around the age of two to three years old. Regression was notably absent from Cameron. He simply hadn't reached milestones. The primary driver of concern was his severe developmental delay, his inattention to people talking or engaging with him, and the new behavior of banging his head in moments of frustration or being upset.

There is definitely a moment that stands out more than any other for me. It's the point that I figuratively threw my hands in the air and checked out. Cameron was about a year and half old, and we took him to get a haircut. It was the worst experience possible. After we spent much time coaxing him to come into a strange hair shop, he finally sat in the chair with reluctance. The moment the clippers were placed on his head he had a meltdown the likes of which we had never seen, crying inconsolably and flailing himself against the chair he was sitting in. The place was crowded, and everyone stared at him. It was all I could do to keep my composure, get Cameron, and head for home. I had no idea what caused his reaction and certainly didn't have the context that I have today. Today's knowledge brings a new perspective on that moment, and I can only imagine what Cam was going through at that time with all of the sensory sensitivities he had.

From a personal perspective, my career was beginning to

take off, as I was promoted into a management role during this time. We were beginning to settle into life as a family of four. I lived only two miles from work, so I was able to come home for lunch, which was always a nice break to the day. From a financial perspective, I was able to provide for my family without Lisa having to work, and for the first time in a long time, I did not have to work two jobs either, which was definitely a win-win!

Over that year and a half, we had settled in as a family and entered a normalizing phase as a family. My schedule at work was the same each week, which provided a layer of stability at home. We were home, healthy, and happy, which is always great. We were growing very close to my in-laws, Tim and Lollie. They were spending a lot of time at the house, and on Sunday afternoons our house became the standard place for dinner, football, and the occasional game of Madden NFL on the PlayStation. We were near a world-renowned trout fishing location, White River, so we spent a lot of spare time fishing the river as well.

My feelings for Cameron had not changed at all, though I kept that information to myself. It wasn't exactly a secret, I am sure. I made no attempt to get to know him, as all I saw were the challenges he presented. The experiences I remember with him all ended up with frustrations. It sounds horrible to say this, but I truly wanted nothing to do with him and did not make any effort to change. There was no way I was going to say anything about my feelings for him, however. It was a very odd feeling not to like my own child yet at the same time know that it wasn't right to feel that way. I plugged fully into Mya during that time. She was daddy's girl, and she knew it.

Moving Away from Home

Walmart was expanding grocery operations in the northwestern U.S., and I was approached with an opportunity to move out there. Going there was virtually a guarantee of a promotion in pretty short order and would mean a lot from a financial security standpoint for my family. Lisa and I discussed it at some length and decided it was the right thing to do.

Looking back on those conversations I realize how reluctant Lisa was to go. She went along with it to appease me. We weren't far removed from our move to Corpus Christi that proved to be challenging financially. As well, we were home. In my heart I knew this move would be different, as the same type of financial struggles would not exist with this move.

The relocation to Idaho was great from an experience standpoint. It is amazing country up there in the panhandle just about seventy miles from the Canadian border. I grossly underestimated how much we would miss home, though. There is nothing like the holidays to bring that longing out in a very real way. Going to eat at a restaurant for Christmas dinner was a lonely experience. It was absolutely beautiful country, but it wasn't the right place for us at that time. I searched for promotional opportunities that were closer to home and found one in Iowa. We would be close enough to home to make the occasional weekend trip. Eight hours away was a far cry from being a two-and-a-half-day journey away. I applied for the position, interviewed, and was offered the role.

We would relocate to Iowa in February 2004. Cameron was two and a half at the time, and Mya was four. Cameron was demonstrating some significant developmental delays at that time. He was still not sleeping through the night, averaging only a few hours of sleep nightly, he had not uttered an intelligible word, and wasn't close to being interested in being potty trained. He experienced meltdowns with run-of-the-mill, routine trips to the store. He did find unique ways of communicating his wants and needs. Though he was unable to talk, he would take one of our hands and put it on the refrigerator when he was thirsty and wanted juice or on the pantry when he wanted a snack.

Cameron was becoming intolerant of high-sensory-engaging environments. It didn't matter whether it was Walmart, a mall, or McDonald's. Each was met with the same result: Cameron became intolerant, went into meltdown phase. and then showed increased levels of frustration with my wife and I as we tried to shuffle him out of the store while avoiding the inquisitive looks of folks around us. Experiencing those events has changed the way I react today when I hear a child crying in a sensory-rich environment. I never look in the direction of a crying child in a store, as I never want to upset a new parent who quite possibly could be dealing with the same thing we did.

In discussion with a neighbor we learned of a service that helped with advice on how to care for a child showing significant delays. I called the service, desperate to improve the situation, as it was becoming a point of serious concern for Lisa. I don't recall the name of the service, but I do remember the phone call. It was clear the person I spoke with knew what she was talking about when she asked me questions about Cameron. From sleepless nights to his behavior and diet, she asked a series of pointed questions, to which my every response was "Yes."

I asked about autism, the person handling the intake call was very quick to point out that the service didn't offer diagnosis, only suggestions for in-home therapy sessions; however, it started with a hearing test. This approach was new, and it made sense, because one of the concerns with Cameron was his being unaware of people engaging with him. Could it have been as simple as being unable to hear?

The hearing test revealed no issues with his ability to hear, so we continued down the path of searching for solutions. The service started coming by the house and introduced what we now know as picture exchange to help Cameron communicate with us. In lieu of having to throw our hand toward the cabinet holding the thing he wanted, he could simply communicate that by showing us a picture. The folks from the service never said anything about autism, only remained proactive in finding solutions to help curb undesired behavior and assist in communication. The picture exchange helped Cameron begin to communicate, and he took to it rapidly. The other difficult behavior did not wane, though. Sleepless nights continued, and we stopped going places as a family, as it was easier for one of us to stay home with Cameron instead of taking him into a sensory-stimulating environment. We tried diligently to keep life normal for Mya – doing that meant doing it with only one of us, however.

From a career standpoint I was definitely on the fast track to achieving my personal goals. In the back of my mind there was a nagging thought that we weren't in the right place from a family-need perspective. I was in a tough store and spending a lot of time at work, 60-70 hours a week were commonplace and sometimes upwards of 80 hours. Lisa was at home with a very needy two-year-old and trying to keep life normal for our three-and-a-half-year-old daughter. While dealing with Cameron was taxing on all of us, Lisa was taking the brunt of it. My time at home did not include any real help with Cameron, as I was still separated emotionally from him. Additionally, for the most part I was unaware of how much support she needed from me during that time. The demands at work were significant. At times I wouldn't see my family for three or four days, because I came home after they went to bed and left before they woke up. In conversation with friends and family I compared it to being a long-haul truck driver, feeling like I had been gone for three days, even though I was going home and sleeping in my own bed.

I was falling apart, and my nerves were shot. I was fighting a two-headed monster; one called job issues and the other called family issues. It was unsustainable, and I began to explore options that would place us in the environment we needed and allow me to be more involved at home. Admitting defeat was not something I did easily, and it was very difficult for me to open up and share my situation with the human resources manager for our region, Gene Tabor. This was another moment in time where God placed me in front of someone whom I would interact with later in life. Though in that moment, Gene was the decision maker for helping us navigate a difficult time in our life, our paths would cross before the decade was over and he would become a lifelong mentor and friend.

Deep inside I knew I was in a situation that I had to get out of. My mother-in-law had already had to come up and stay with us for several days – this happened a few times in a short amount of time. She was there to support Lisa – a role I should have been in. I finally opened up at work and shared the challenges we were having and was offered a couple of options. The quickest option was to step down one level and go to a store that was about three hours from home. Because that solution was the quickest, I took it, and in 2004 we headed back to central Arkansas, a mere three hours from home. Little did I know I was going from the furnace into the fire.

WARNING: Rough Times Ahead

Although we were closer to home, the challenges profession-ally grew. I had leapt from the furnace into the fire. My time at work did not decrease at all, and my time away from home was even more, because of the commute. With the voluntary demotion came a negative impact to our income. To offset it we chose to live outside of the city in a more affordable com-munity. The result was an hour drive into work. I was strug-gling to hold it all together. Everything was crumbling around me, and nothing was going as planned. Internally I was strug-gling with my decision to step down. It didn't matter that I knew it was for the right reasons, my point of focus was what I had lost. Not only had my career progress and plans been set back, but I also had no clue what was next.

Admittedly this was the point when I really began to re-sent Cameron. I blamed him for the challenges he brought into our family. I looked at him as the reason we were strug-gling financially. I looked at him as the reason there was so much tension in the house, because of his inability to sleep during the night or handle social situations. I accepted zero responsibility for my actions and took a selfish vantage point when evaluating the situation. My resentments formed a wedge between my wife and me and my son and me.

It's odd, really, the clouded judgment discontent can create. The pride of being a good husband and dad wasn't top of mind anymore. The company I loved to work for became a thorn in my side. I took a downward spiral into a very bad place. I faced a daily struggle with constant blame and victim mentality. I was wholly unhappy, and I can only imagine what I was like to be around.

My personal life was an absolute wreck. I had been a casual smoker since I was sixteen smoking about a half pack of cigarettes a day, but I began to smoke more than ever, more than a pack a day, as smoking became a way to blow off steam, a coping mechanism. I didn't smoke in the house, so smoking became a way to separate myself and exit the premises. I had unhealthy eating habits that became even worse. My day was filled with one soda after another. I'd go through about a twelve-pack every two to three days. I ate feel-good foods—pastries for breakfast and a bowl of ice cream nightly.

The net result was a significant increase in weight over the previous year. I had gone from a size thirty-six waist to a forty-four as I piled on more than ninety pounds without hardly noticing. I was unhappy, though I didn't call it depression. Looking back on it I can say without doubt I was in a very dark place. It's surprising how quickly one can become consumed by negativity and unhappiness. Life became centered on my unhappiness, and I searched for anything to make the situation better.

I made a series of bad decisions in a continuous grasp to find momentary glimpses of accomplishment and happiness. The first was to buy a home. It was 2005 and mortgage lenders were more than happy to stretch people to their absolute maximum, or even beyond their maximum, to get a house deal secured. We found a house a little closer to work and went through the much-too-easy process of buying it. Although there is great pride in buying a home, as it is a symbol of the American dream, this decision was not sound at all. It tightened the financial requirements we had, although we were barely making it.

Things were eroding at home. The miserable attitude toward life I projected daily had to be very difficult for Lisa to handle. Cameron was two and a half and we were still learning how to best deal with his significant delays and behavior issues. By then we were growing increasingly confident that his issue was autism. Unfortunately, no one would diagnose autism until the child is three. To compound the issues, there was a substantial waiting list of from six to nine months at the only place in the state where we could get a diagnosis. After pleading with our doctor at one of Cameron's routine appointments, we were finally able to get on the list to get an appointment for a formal diagnosis. Although Cameron was not yet three years old, because of the wait time, he would be three at the time of the appointment. The appointment was set for March of the following year, nine seemingly long months away.

I came home one day from work and Lisa said the words that no man ever wants to hear. It was a confrontation about our relationship and where we were, which was on the fast track to divorce. I can imagine she had felt that way for some time, and it had finally gotten to a point where she couldn't avoid saying something.

I was stubborn and I did not believe her. I told her I would fight her for Mya, but she could keep Cameron. It was perhaps the most self-absorbed thing I had ever said, but I was fighting a deep-seated disdain for Cameron, completely centered on blame for our personal situation, as if I had no fault in the situation. When she told me she was going to take the kids and stay with her mom and dad for a while, I realized the gravity of the situation around me. I convinced her to let me take a couple days off work and see if she and I could go out of town. Sadly, the madness of the last couple of years had not allowed us to have a single date. I am thankful she agreed, and I was able to take a couple days off to attempt a recalibration. While it was good, it would ultimately be a temporary reprieve, only to return to the same, even worsening situation.

There isn't an overnight fix to a deep-seated issue two years in the making. I did not approach with enthusiasm going back to work that Monday morning after having four days off. I wasn't happy with life in general, and in that state, challenges that arise compound the situation. Normal situations that one might brush off become sticking, insurmountable points, which is exactly what happened that Monday morning when our district manager walked in. Up until then, he and I had a great relationship, but apparently he didn't agree with my taking a few days off. He had a unique way of being passive-aggressive that, on that day, was too much for me to deal with. The first thing he did, in the most condescending and uncaring way possible, was ask me if everything was okay, or if I needed a few more days off. Trust me when I say it was not from a position of caring. Rather it was his way of letting me know he didn't like my being away.

Perhaps any other day I would have brushed off his comment and gone about my day, but it didn't sit well with me at all. Although we had gone our separate ways that morning, he was still around the store, and I decided it was worth having a conversation with him. I hoped the conversation would accomplish two things; first, confront reality and be able to let him know how I felt about my personal situation being diminished, and second, let him know I was struggling with an ever-devolving personal situation that was heavily impacting my professional life. I sought him out when he was by himself and asked if he had a few minutes to chat.

His response was terse, "There are twenty-two people in front of you. Get in line." And he turned and walked away.

I was done. At that moment I decided it was time for me to find a different career path.

That day on lunch break I perused the newspaper and saw a classified ad for a door-to-door food delivery service. It offered income potential that was greater than my current income. Could that job be what made everything right? I certainly saw it that way and went through the company's hiring process over the next few days. As luck (stay tuned) would have it, I was offered the position. I gave Walmart a half days' notice, and I was on my way. It took all of about one week to determine I had made perhaps one of the most shortsighted decisions of my life.

Immediately I saw that my income was trending to be about half of what it was. Sure, potential was there, but it depended on every customer buying from me, and that was about as likely as being struck by lightning twice. I didn't say anything to Lisa until I had to, the first paycheck, two weeks in. I felt the weight of the world on my shoulders as I tried to explain how we would be okay, even though I knew we wouldn't. The hours I was working made the option of working a second job impossible. With two small kiddos at home and one who had significant behavior problems, although we didn't know what yet, we were a one-income family, and my family's well-being depended on every decision I made. In one decision I had placed everything at risk and turned my back on a great career.

That weekend my in-laws had planned to come over, and when they arrived, Lisa and I did our best to put on a happy face. Our cupboards were bare, as we didn't have much money to buy groceries that week, and were still figuring out what in the world we were going to do. My father-in-law, Tim, looked at me and said, "C'mon. We are going to the store to get you all some food." We went to the store and he loaded up a basket of groceries. They never asked about our situation, but they knew. Some years later we would discuss that moment, and apparently my mother-in-law, Lollie, went to get something from the pantry, saw how little we had, and pulled Tim aside and told him. As a man it is hard to describe how it feels to have someone buy you something because you need it. I was thankful beyond measure, as it provided a solution for the short term, but it was incredibly difficult to face the fact that my in-laws had to buy my family food because of my shortsighted decision.

Back on Track, Kind of...

I don't believe in chance or fate. No doubt God was looking over our situation and intervened at a most critical time. I was entering my third week with my new employer, frantically looking for an exit strategy, but completely lost. It weighed heavily on my mind day and night as I realized that I had put my family between a rock and a hard place. My sales route was very rural, particularly in the mornings, and cell phone reception in those areas was pathetic at that time.

It's funny to look back on those days of roaming charges and how far the industry has come. I kept my phone off, most of the time when I was out in the sticks, because I had no service and there wasn't a point in draining my battery. As I came back into town for the afternoon portion of my route, I pulled the truck over and started eating the peanut butter and jelly sandwich I'd packed for the day. I flipped the phone on and heard the tone of a voicemail message, one I will never forget.

I checked my message, and it was the familiar voice of Cameron Davis, the manager who hired me and promoted me so many years previously. To this day I still remember the contents of that message. *"John, it's Cameron Davis. I want to talk to you about an opportunity. You may be completely done with this company and want nothing to do with it, but if you're interested, give me a call."*

The message was really great to hear, but I was a bit confused. How did Cameron know that I left the company? I knew word traveled faster than email sometimes, but I hadn't talked to Cameron in a couple of years, so I couldn't figure out how he even knew I had quit. Nevertheless, I was *definitely* interested in whatever he had to say and immediately returned his call.

It turns out Keith, one of the managers I had previously worked for, stopped at the post office in Gassville, Arkansas, to buy stamps on his way home from work one day, and wouldn't you know it, my father-in-law was the postmaster at that location. He happened to be working the front desk that afternoon. Keith and Tim knew each other from the time I had worked with him. Keith was an avid fisherman, as we were. In casual conversation, Keith asked how I was doing, and Tim told him that I had quit the company and the challenges that led up to my quitting. Keith, of course, had told Cameron.

I called Cameron back immediately and discovered that Walmart was expanding back in my hometown and was looking for a manager with a unique skillset–specifically someone with a strong grocery background. I told Cameron I was definitely interested. He put me in touch with the district manager at the location, and within the span of forty-five minutes over lunch that day I had a job offer to be reinstated with the company and relocated back home. All I asked for was a few minutes to call Lisa and discuss it with her. Although I knew it was a foregone conclusion that we would accept, we had the matter of a house we owned—or the bank owned it, and we just made the payments—and we were not sure how to handle that encumbrance.

After some brief discussion with Tim and Lollie, who we leaned heavily on for insight and wisdom during that time, we decided to put the house on the market. We would move in with them for a short time while we hoped to sell our house. By the end of that week we were on our way back home. My employment had been restored, I was being reinstated, and it was an opportunity to reset the clock on my career and be home.

The story doesn't end there, though, as I was not finished making mistakes. Things were about to get interesting with life in general.

The next several months brought a sense of normalcy back to the Leachman household. For the first couple of months we lived with my in-laws, Tim and Lollie, as we hoped to sell our house. There weren't any nibbles on it, and rightfully so. We had overpaid for it, and it was not in a favorable location. At that point we decided to explore renting the house, as co-dwelling—one family of two and one family of four—was not optimal. It served a short-term gap, but had its challenges.

We put an ad in the paper to rent our house and within a few days had several calls. One couple was very interested, and we met them there to look at the house. They were about to get married and the house would be their first home. By the end of the visit they decided they wanted it, and we signed the papers. We finally had a bit of financial relief with the payments being covered by the rent checks. Within a couple weeks we found a three-bedroom apartment of our own just seven miles from my work. It was well timed, because my father-in-law had just accepted a promotion to the state offices, and he and Lollie would be relocating to Little Rock. The irony was that just a few months after we moved home, they were moving to where we came from.

Life was on the uptick as things began to feel somewhat normal for me professionally. My relationship with Cameron had not changed much. I was very much on the sidelines in terms of being a dad to him. After a couple years of not investing in any type of relationship, I didn't have any feelings, and I was indifferent to him. Most of my time as a dad was spent with Mya, who was about to start pre-school.

Cameron was still demonstrating significant delays and not developing at the pace he should. At the age of three he had still not spoken his first word, seemed indifferent to conversation in his direction, and showed no interest in even beginning to be potty trained. He started demonstrating some other strong signals of autism, too, with a very strong tendency of order - such as lining up his toy cars or cans of fruits and vegetables. Everything had to have a specific order or structure to it.

In an interesting twist, his necessity to create order around himself was the very beginning of a glimmer of interaction between Cameron and me. As he ran out of the room to get one of his cars to continue the line, I would remove one from the middle and put the like back together to try to trick him. It didn't matter how long the line of cars or cans were, within seconds of running back into the room he would look for the missing car. I'd reveal it from behind my back, and he'd grab it and put it in line. We'd repeat that process as long as he was willing to play. It was the first time I recall looking at the situation from his perspective and meeting him where he needed to be met.

The Official Diagnosis

We were approaching the time of his appointment for a diagnosis at the Dennis Developmental Center, near the Arkansas Children's Hospital. We never talked about it as a couple. In many ways Lisa and I were dealing with the diagnosis in our own ways. Although we went through all the early stages of denial, I am grateful we never let it delay our choice to get Cameron diagnosed, as recommended by his doctor. As hard as it was to face the possibility that we would hear that Cameron had something wrong with him, we always walked forward, knowing it was important to allow the evaluation to play out.

In my time since that diagnosis I am still shocked at how many parents allow the issue of evaluation to become a sticking point. I can say with 100 percent certainty that if someone is letting pride or fear get in the way of an evaluation, it is only making a challenging situation worse. To people who have been unwilling to take that step because they don't think their child has a problem, my advice is look at it from the vantage point of proving the professionals wrong. So you go down there and get the evaluation and it comes back the way you thought it would. Great! However, what if the doctors are right? What if there is something wrong? Every day, every week is time wasted that could be used for potential progress.

After nine long months of waiting, the day of the evaluation arrived. It was a completely miserable experience. It was a full day of surveys and tests that I will never forget. Handing Cameron over to the team of medical professionals on that day was the first day that I felt bad for him. He was off in a room being observed, and we were filling out a battery of surveys for parental input.

At the end of the day we gathered around a small conference table, and the words *autism spectrum disorder* rolled off the tongues of the panel. Panel members handed us a large pile of handouts and information to sift through and make sense of.

We got business cards for the people, but it became painfully obvious that we were an often and quick occurrence for them, and they did not want to become a lifetime resource. We discovered that information in short order.

One instance that stands out more than most in those early days was Cameron's behavior problems at pre-K. We got the "Your son bit another child today" note once. The situation revealed the isolation we would soon feel for some time. In one way it brought to light the lack of understanding from other parents about our child's condition. Lisa felt horrible about what Cameron had done, and even though the school would never tell the parent who bit their child, she felt it appropriate to apologize to the mother. She was made to feel miserable for the situation, even though she had absolutely no influence or control over it.

At the same time it was shortly after the diagnosis that I called one of the psychologists whose business card I had. We were desperate and craving information about how to help Cameron and what we could do. The diagnosis team clearly felt its responsibility ended at the point of diagnosis and the pamphlet it provided. I was told in no uncertain terms that it was not its job to handle individual cases, and we were supposed to find someone locally who could help. The walls of isolation began to close in. It felt like an island; we had nowhere to go to find anyone who had walked in my shoes and on whom we could lean for some advice or recommendation. We were in a small town, and resources were limited. Everything catered to more of a generalist approach.

The feeling is odd, really, that one can have child with autism, a disorder that at the time had CDC stats of one in 250 kids being diagnosed as being on the autism spectrum, and still feel completely alone, but that is exactly how I felt. What I learned is that all too often it's just easier to live your life at home. Public spaces are *hard* for parents with high-need kids, no matter the age. People constantly judge your child and your parenting style when the inevitable meltdown occurs. No one I talked to was helpful, and I soon found out that society as a whole has its own idea of what autism is.

In particular I would have loved to have some perspective from another dad dealing with the same issues. Everything I found, from books to websites, seemed to be from a mother's perspective. I didn't find a lot of help in those places, because men and women come at things from separate angles.

And then there was the inevitable frustration of dealing with the general public's lack of understanding of autism. People's point of view at that time was what they had learned from Hollywood. I got exhausted from answering the question, "What's his special skill?" I wanted to reply, "Sleepless nights and picky eating habits," but I always tried to find some way of just getting out of the conversation.

Looking back at that time now, I know that it was far too much about me—what I had supposedly lost—than it was about Cameron and what he had to gain. I let myself wallow in self-pity far too long, but I felt robbed, and the feelings of blame were strong. He was my son, my future Arkansas Razorback football player, my future Dallas Cowboy, the boy I was supposed to take hunting and fishing and do man stuff with. Suddenly those dreams would not be possible.

I placed limits on Cameron and what he could or would achieve. It's sad to admit, but I defined him by his limits instead of focusing on what he needed in order to overcome them. I was thrust back into the darkness of unhappiness, the same world that led to a series of mistakes and the same that would lead me down a series of more.

After we got the diagnosis for Cameron, the wheels of logic began to turn in my head. You know how men are. We like to tinker with things and fix them. Likewise, and an all-too-familiar habit up to that point, I didn't talk about any of my thoughts and feelings with Lisa.

We had enrolled Cameron in a local early childhood program in our hometown that provided the therapy that he needed. Cameron had the high need for steady and frequent sessions of speech, occupational, and physical therapy. He received speech therapy from two sources.

To that end, one thing I remain eternally grateful for are the early people, teachers, and therapists who were and continue to be placed in our lives. Everyone engaged with Cameron approached the situation with a determined attitude. What I remember most about the early days of enrollment and meetings to discuss therapy services was the focus on what he *could* do, versus what he couldn't, which was a completely different way of thinking for me at that time. My mind and days were filled with focusing on the limitations of autism and Cam and certainly not centered on anything other than what he couldn't do then and wouldn't be able to do. Perhaps in small ways the work of the therapists was helping shape my mindset on proactive thinking and action, regardless of the impending mistakes.

As I surveyed the situation internally, I convinced myself that our situation was not the best for Cameron. If I'm being honest, it was more about me continually and consistently searching for something, anything new, for moments of happiness. I was still dealing with a significant amount of blame and self-pity. I hadn't come to grips with moving forward because I was stuck looking in the rearview mirror focused mostly on what I didn't have. Something new would bring the mundane moments and dealing with the reality of the situation at bay.

Lisa's parents were relocating to Little Rock. Oh, the irony in that situation! We had just left Little Rock, and they were headed down there for Tim's new position with the post office. Add to that a new wrinkle to deal with. The rent checks had abruptly stopped coming in. It had been two months since the last check from the folks who were renting our house and phone calls had gone unreturned. We feared the worst.

Lisa and I made a trip to discover the house had, indeed, been abandoned. Thankfully it was in decent shape and needed few repairs. The situation was going to put immediate pressure on our finances, though.

Another Move?

The combination of two events–Cameron's increasing need for additional services and the fact that we were very close to losing our home because we were unable to make both a rent and house payment–brought me to the conclusion that we should move back to Little Rock. The house that was being abandoned provided the perfect excuse for me to validate (to myself) that we needed to move back. I never even considered putting it back on the rental market. I was laser focused on embracing something new to take my mind off the reality I was unwilling to face. I convinced myself that moving to Little Rock was exactly what we had to do. It would be different this time, I surmised, as Lisa's parents were there, and I centered my decision on getting services for Cameron and being financially secure.

I made one critical error. I kept my reasoning internal and never once spoke to Lisa about it. I know it sounds ridiculous, and it absolutely was, but without ever discussing it with Lisa, I began the process of seeking a transfer to the Little Rock area, although in a different market than I was previously in. I knew she wouldn't want to move, but at the same time I was completely convinced that it was what we needed to do. Trust me, as much as you are shaking your head right now, trying to understand my logic, I am shaking mine as I write, thinking back to that time. But just wait, it gets much worse.

As if it wasn't bad enough that I made a major life-change decision without considering Lisa's point of view, the manner in which I chose to relay the news to her was even worse. I knew that I needed to talk to her about it, but I avoided the confrontation, because I knew where it would lead. After I had finalized the details of the transfer–dates and timing–I began my final week at my then-current location. Lisa took the kids into their preschools, as was the typical routine, and I was going in to work a little later in the morning. After she left, I wrote a letter that I would leave on the oven for her to discover when she came home. I explained the rationale I used to make the decision that we were going to relocate to Little Rock and that ultimately the decision had been made and was final.

I received her call later that morning at work. It was the toughest conversation I've ever navigated. I don't know if she was more shocked than she was upset or more upset than she was shocked, but it was a healthy mixture of both. Why or how she made that trip with me is a mystery, but it definitely speaks to the woman she is. While I was making the situation 100 percent about me in a very selfish manner, she remained completely selfless, regardless of how much she disagreed with the situation and decision. She was demonstrating to me exactly what I wasn't willing to do for my son. Lisa remained focused on the good in me instead of focusing on my mistakes or misjudgments

We moved back to Little Rock, and I started work in the new location. While the new market was a much-improved working situation than I previously had in the local area, it was not without its challenges, both personally and professionally.

A few months prior to our relocating, I had upgraded my truck from one that was paid for to one that came with a monthly payment. I was at that time riding a wave of financial relief with the house being rented. The new work location was a considerable distance from where we lived, though, so the essence of living paycheck to paycheck crept back into the conversation.

Mya started kindergarten that year, and we enrolled her in a school near the house. Cameron's autism-specific preschool was by my work location, so I took him, and Lisa picked him up later that afternoon. He got out in time for her to pick him up and then get to the school to pick up Mya. The result of all of this commuting was lots of fuel consumption. We had an SUV and a truck, so fuel mileage was not on our side. Lisa searched for a part-time job that would offer her the chance to work in the mornings after dropping Cameron off. It was a robust job market, and she was able to find something pretty quickly. It made the difference between us sinking or keeping our heads above water, for sure. It also added a considerable amount of stress in the house. Trying to coordinate schedules and lengthy round-trip travel to drop off and pick up Cam on my days off from work made what once seemed like a logical conclusion become illogical.

Cameron also started getting routine ear infections during

that time. Trips to the doctor were absolutely miserable, as he quickly associated them with poking, prodding, and the inevitable shot of Rocephyn. It was taxing on Cameron and whoever was with him. Even the simple routine process of taking his temperature required holding his arms to his side and in place while the clinician put a thermometer in his ear. The shot offered another situation in which I had to physically hold Cameron down while someone administered the shot. Each of these moments fueled my frustration.

Absent were concerns about what Cameron might be going through. I never considered the sensory issues at the root of the behavior–that it was physically taxing on him to endure such a thing. No, what I saw in those days was a kid who was just hell to deal with. During one particularly rough visit, his doctor planted a seed. I still remember the exact moment and the words he said. "You all are going through one of the hardest times that you will ever go through with Cameron," he said. "As much as you are learning how to have a young child with autism, he is trying to learn how to be a young child with autism, and one day, though you don't see it now, it will all feel normal, for both of you." It was the first time that someone spoke of seeing the situation from Cameron's point of view rather than from mine.

I began to explore autism a little more and take an interest in Cameron's environment at school. In learning about some of his activities he engaged in at school, I found parallels to his early days as a toddler. He still *loved* to swing, and the school had several styles, from swaddling to platform. Each offered him the opportunity to engage in the sensory-rich activity. At home we didn't have anything that offered something similar, indoors or out, so I bought a swing that could be mounted to the ceiling. He absolutely loved it! He got so good at it that he could run from the other room and leap into it, which caused the swing to go in a circular pattern around the room. He frequented that swing daily.

In the span of less than nine months Lisa and I were approaching a similar feeling–we were growing further and further apart and both kind of coexisting under the same roof. Though we lived only about twenty miles from her parents, it might as well had been two hundred miles. Our hectic schedules and demands of life resulted in very few visits to their house or their visits to ours. Yes, everything that I had intended to fix, everything I had convinced myself would change because of the move, was accomplishing the complete opposite.

But wait! There's more. Financial stress was setting in because of a really dumb decision. Mya had a birthday in June, and we knew that financially we would be unable to get her anything. When you are living paycheck to paycheck, it doesn't take much to throw the situation into disarray. The electric bill had been unusually high for a couple of months, and we were running a little behind on the truck payment. The combination of bills higher than expected plus late fees created a shortfall in our finances. As I looked over the bills that month, desperately searching for a solution that offered some additional resources for a gift, it became clear that all the usual tricks had run their course and there was nothing extra. Worthless: that's the best word I can think of to describe the feeling I had for not being able to provide for my daughter's birthday and knowing in the deepest part of my heart that it was absolutely my fault.

Behold! Right next to where I worked was a payday loan place. I went in to see what the details were and discovered that I was eligible for up to a $900 payday advance. The fee for the short-term loan would be dependent on what I borrowed but make no mistake; it was far from nominal, regardless of the amount. It offered me the opportunity to feel like a hero for the day, though, and that, I concluded, was worth any cost, so I did it. I procured a $300 payday advance that would come with a $360 payback in two weeks. I would deal with the payback when the time came. Right then I didn't want to think about it.

I went to Walmart with $300 to spend. It was the first time in several months that we had been any extra money, even though it was far from legitimately extra. I picked up what we wanted to get Mya and I stopped by housewares to get a blender. Lisa had been talking about wanting to make smoothies, but we didn't own a blender. I completed the shopping trip with some strawberries, bananas, and smoothie mix. Walking in the house that afternoon I felt great. Lisa was excited about her blender and Mya was going to have something to open on her birthday. Lisa asked how I had done it, and I explained in ways that lacked the details of the high-interest payback. Nonetheless, everything was good–if only for a couple of weeks.

Paying back the payday loan prompted an interesting challenge. We lived paycheck to paycheck, with absolutely nothing left over, so coming up with the $60 to pay the loan was going to create a shortfall. I had borrowed only $300 of the $900 I was eligible for, so an opportunity immediately presented itself. I could borrow $360 to cover the payback fee and be good for a couple of weeks. The payback on the $360 and subsequent fee would surely create another shortfall, but I had plenty of room between the money I had borrowed and the $900 cap, so every two weeks I paid what I borrowed plus the fee and then got an advance to cover that amount. It was a short-term solution, and time was rapidly marching toward the day I would have to take the cap, $900, which came with a whopping payback fee of $189. Yep, you read that right, a two-week advance of $900 with a payback of $1089.

I was hoping that fuel prices would come down, that the electric bill would subside, that anything would happen to allow the gravity of the situation from revealing itself, but those things were not going to happen. It was late summer of 2005 and Hurricane Katrina was about to wreak havoc on the Gulf Coast and fuel prices were about to soar to above three dollars a gallon. The only thing that would provide a shred of relief would be the end of summer and lower electric bills. Gas prices offset any hope of climbing out of the hole I had dug for us. Late fees were mounting up on every bill that was due. My financial distress was extremely high.

On my way to work one morning I heard an ad on the radio about bankruptcy. A local firm was advertising a free consultation and a low price if it were determined that we qualified and wanted to pursue. I had no idea what bankruptcy was, but I had an idea and thought it was worth learning more. I set an appointment and decided that we would best pursue the payback option, chapter seven, that would allow us to keep our house and vehicles. I would have a large percentage of money taken out of my paycheck and distributed to all creditors. It seemed like a reasonable and fair way to approach the situation.

We discovered that year that Cameron had an affinity for breaking glass. I was busy in the other room but kept hearing a strange noise that I couldn't identify, but it wasn't overly concerning, so I kept working on whatever I was working on. When I later rounded the corner and went into the living room, I found that Cameron had discovered that if he threw the Christmas ornaments on the ceramic tile near the front door they shattered into hundreds of pieces, an activity he apparently took great pleasure in. What complicated the matter was that he had apparently bitten into at least one of the ornaments, because he had a couple pieces stuck to his chin. We didn't know whether he had swallowed any of it, and if so, how big the piece was. Yep, you guessed it, a trip to the hospital was in order.

There is one thing worse than a trip to the ER, and that's a trip to the ER at bedtime with a child who is moderately to severely autistic. The personnel are not in a hurry for anyone, and the receptionist looked at us with a blank stare when we asked for somewhere quiet to wait, because the noise was getting to Cameron. After four hours, the hospital staff determined there were no foreign objects in Cam's tummy or intestines. We had an ornament-less Christmas that year and rejoiced gleefully when the industry transitioned to the shatterproof variety the following year.

While I experienced fleeting moments of happiness, the old familiar winds were blowing. I was becoming increasingly disenchanted with the circumstance of where we were financially. The old seeds of unhappiness, blame, and despair were starting to sprout. Truthfully, I was refusing to come to grips with life. I had spent the prior three years of my life focused on momentary and temporary happiness—a new location, a new job, a new house, a new truck, a new living location, a blender, and an inflatable pool paid for by a payday loan, just anything because dealing with the reality of life in front of me was far less appealing than something shiny and new. Moreover, I found that change often provided me with an escape from reality for a while, because it created something new to focus on. It was my default switch. When things did not go the way that I wanted them to, I immediately sought momentary satisfaction in something else. It was the exact reason that I was not truly investing in a relationship with my son. I was focused on Cameron's limitations hell bent on blaming him for the entirety of our situation. I always found a way to make him, not me, the common denominator for our situation—the increased medical bills, the need to have him in a special school, etc. I went through the motions of being a provider for him, but I invested little in being a dad to him. Most of my time I thought about me and carried a high degree of unhappiness around with me.

I began to peruse the promotional job opportunities, as I figured it would improve the situation we were in. Although filing for bankruptcy helped keep the creditors at bay, we had very little leftover money, so we were still living very much paycheck to paycheck after the deductions. There were no promotional opportunities available in the local area, but an opportunity presented itself in Williston, North Dakota. It sounded interesting when I explored it more. Of course, I realize now it offered only what I was truly seeking: a change from my circumstances that would take my mind off reality for a little while.

I applied for the job, and, yes, you guessed it; I never said a word about it to Lisa. I convinced myself there wasn't a point in talking about it until I knew I got the job. In reality I was avoiding what I knew would be a very challenging conversation about another relocation. I got a call one day from the hiring manager for the position I had applied for. I had made the initial cut, as they were trimming down the applicant pool. He wanted to interview me. We set a date for a phone interview in a couple of days, and no, I didn't say anything to Lisa. The interview went well, and I felt like I would likely be getting a job offer, but I didn't know for sure. The hiring staff was going to wrap up the interviews in the next seven to ten days and make a decision.

Sure enough, I got a call one day a couple weeks later offering me the position. I emphatically said yes, regardless of the fact that I hadn't said anything to Lisa. There had been many times since I applied that I had intended to have a conversation with her. Each day I eventually did not do it, though, I committed to myself that the next day I would. I knew it would be an emotionally charged conversation and she wouldn't be happy. I didn't expect the conversation to go the way it actually did, however.

Lisa was done, and rightfully so. For years I had invested much more into me than I had in a relationship of consideration for what she might be thinking, feeling, and going through as well. I had kept us in a consistent state of flux as a family. Each time we moved felt to me like it was for the right reasons, but each relocation chipped away at the foundation of Lisa's and my relationship. Our marriage was a mess as one might suspect it would be, after years of not investing anything meaningful into it. I had been far too worried about my own feelings to care much about anyone else's.

This time Lisa said in no uncertain terms that she was not moving and that if I wanted to go, I would make the trip by myself.

That reaction surprised me, although it shouldn't have. I had assumed she would pack up and head north with me, so now what in the world was I going to do? I had already committed to the hiring manager, and I had plans to make a trip up there to find housing in a week. I believed that Lisa was simply upset in the moment and would eventually come to her senses and go along. Yeah, I had the audacity to think that Lisa was the one needing to come to her senses. If that fact doesn't tell you how far removed I was from the situation, not much else will. I continued with my plans to drive up there the following week to explore the local community.

The trip, perhaps the loneliness of the road for hours on end, provided multiple reflection points for me. The evening calls with Lisa offered nothing new. She simply was not budging. What I didn't know but was slowly coming the conclusion of was that it wasn't just about that moment. The distant feeling I heard in her voice or felt in the silence was much more about the state of our marriage and where it was headed. I decided it was time to return home, earlier than I had originally planned, and try to put the pieces back together. I would soon find out that the situation was much more dire than I thought it was.

During the trip home I came to my senses and realized that moving to another state was unreasonable. Moving the family wouldn't result in anything other than being 1,500 miles away from anyone we knew or loved and that it was a short-term solution at best. I got home and told Lisa I had decided that moving would not be best and that we were going to stay put.

What I thought would result in a moment of happiness and relief was anything but. On that day our marriage met the most challenging moment in our young, seven-year journey. Lisa didn't know if she wanted to be with me anymore. All the years of enduring a man that cared more for his own feelings than those of his family had taken its toll. We were worlds apart, and I had failed to recognize the warning signs that were likely there all along. That's the thing about being selfish; it prohibits you from being in tune to what's going on around you.

The next couple of months were painful to endure, as we had an uncertain future. Although we were living under the same roof, we weren't talking. She had asked for space to figure out what she wanted, and I respected her request.

I am thankful for her parents during those times. I know now that she leaned heavily on her mom. Her mom asked her if she still loved me, if there was any love there. When Lisa said yes, her mom told her that the marriage was worth saving and that time and my willingness to change could result in us making it.

I leaned heavily on her dad, as Tim was the only person I

felt I could talk to about our situation. I was unsure of how to approach Lisa, when to engage and when not to. Tim always listened and offered support and advice.

I asked Lisa one day if she would want to move back to what we had always called home, Mountain Home, Arkansas. I told her that if she wanted to do that I would put in for a transfer, because I knew the district manager who had the area. She seemed keen to that idea, so in early 2006 I began to the process of trying to get us back home. It didn't take as long as I thought, and though Lisa and I were still very much trying to grow closer, we were headed back to Mountain Home.

Putting Life Back Together

The year of 2006 was a year of transformation in many ways, some intentional and some not so much. At the advice of Cameron's doctor, we had enrolled him in a day clinic/school where he was receiving occupational, physical, and speech therapy. Although there is a lot of red tape to deal with when you have a special needs child, from forms to fill out to required meetings with the school to discuss goals and approaches, it was actually these very meetings that got gears turning in my head.

I have to hand it special education teachers and therapists, because they are truly special people. They spend their lives dedicated to enriching the lives of those who are less fortunate.

I am an analytical person, in part because I'm inquisitive, but in larger part because I am a bit of a debater. I love to challenge the moment, whatever moment I am in and enjoy a good mental sparring session. The meetings that we attended for Cameron always included an update on his progress. What stood out to me, more than anything else, was the true joy that therapists and teachers got from watching their accomplishments. For example, the speech therapist, Bernadette, smiled and clapped with true and genuine joy when Cameron reached a milestone with her and demonstrated the same behavior at home. I imagined that she was demonstrating the same joy as watching a child walk for the first time.

When it comes to addressing symptoms, in many ways autism doesn't differ from the common cold or allergies. Opinions, medically based or otherwise, come from everywhere. It's important to put a disclaimer here. When I say the things that didn't work for Cameron, that's exactly what I am saying. All parents/caregivers owe it to themselves and their kiddos to explore alternative treatment methods that may work. You might just find they do, which is wonderful news. For us, however, none of the things we tried worked. We explored toxin-removing clays, we did the gluten-free/casein-free diets, and heavy antioxidant drinks. We even considered hyperbaric oxygen therapy as a means of making things better.

I became cynical toward things advertised to allegedly work for autism. I became keenly aware very early on that we were a convenient and vulnerable consumer market.

We had a son with autism and were desperately seeking solutions. Cue the money-hungry vultures offering quick solutions and "cures." If I could offer one piece of advice to someone new to the autism world, it would be to look at everything with a skeptical approach and realize your child is someone else's paycheck. Today's world offers even more connectivity than Lisa and I were exposed to. Social media is a great way to connect parents with others beyond the boundaries of city limits. Take advantage of that! Explore other parents' perspectives on alternative forms of treatment. Parents are brutally honest and raw with feedback. Seek it out!

I have an unpopular opinion, all my own. In the very early days, I felt that autism was an overused term. While on one hand it helped people understand, many times I felt that it furthered the gap of understanding. Shows on TV and movies featuring autism focused on socially awkward geniuses. That's not Cameron, nor will it ever be, yet shows like those furthered the divide of Joe Public's understanding of what autism is and what it isn't.

Perhaps my perspective filter changed, but it certainly seemed that autism was trendy, for lack of a better word, in the early 2000s. It's what I both love and hate about that time period and all points forward. In one way it brought autism to the fore and helped people kind of understand it–or at least accept it—for which I am grateful.

If you've never experienced someone moderately to severely autistic, there simply isn't a good way to explain it, especially when the only context filter one has is a TV show or movie they saw. This is one of the primary reasons I have been very open on social media about Cameron's plight. My goal today is to bring people into his world, his challenges, and by default our challenges, to shed light on the many faces of autism.

One of the more involved things we took part in was a study with a doctor from the Arkansas Children's Hospital who was studying oxidative stress in children with autism. We explored it a bit with our doctor and decided that even though it was highly involved and a bit invasive, it was worth exploring further. It was free to participate in, and it differed from the things I mentioned earlier. The other things promised results, and this offered only exploration based on a thesis.

I can offer a very layperson description of the study. At its core, the study centered on the body's ability to rid itself of toxins by examining the levels of glutathione, an antioxidant, in the blood. I cannot even recall how we heard about the study, but we took a trip to Children's Hospital to meet with the doctor. Lisa and I were super impressed with the care and concern the doctor demonstrated. Aside from Cameron's pediatrician, she was the first person we interacted with post-diagnosis who talked to us on a level we understood and yet still in a comprehensive way.

We also sensed an underlying hope that I did not recall ever feeling before. Yes, the study was a trial, and that point was made abundantly clear to us throughout all phases of communication with the doctor and her assistant. That said, it was difficult not to allow my mind to wander and look at it as the thing that would cure Cameron. Oh, how I wanted something that would restore his mind and allow him to be our version of normal. I suppose it is natural for those wishes to happen, regardless of the warnings to temper expectations.

The test had several components, each requiring action from us. Certainly the most time consuming was keeping notes in a daily journal. The process was manual, meaning pen and paper. Every day we jotted down notes on Cameron's behavior, demeanor, and mood. We gathered intel from the therapists he was seeing to make sure we had a good picture of his overall day.

In addition, we had to do a few things either every day or

every few days. The least invasive was giving him a daily folic acid supplement. Every few days we had to give him an injection of methyl b12. If I recall correctly, we gave him smaller doses at first, building up to the full injection amount. Last, there was a twenty-minute Epsom salt bath every few days. The bath routine was always fun, I say with a smirk. Cameron wasn't much for baths at the time, and he certainly wasn't much for patience, so the combination of both having to take a bath *and* having to sit in there for twenty minutes was challenging. Lisa and I traded off on this one. We would invent new ways to keep him entertained and take his mind off the fact that he was taking a bath.

The net result for us was twofold. First, and most disappointing to us, we saw no change in Cam's behavior. On the whole he pretty much remained the same over the duration of the study; however, Lisa and I learned a significant thing from taking part in this test, information that we still use today. The discipline of charting Cameron's behavior revealed some interesting correlations to things we had not noticed before. We noticed a pattern of changed behavior, be it rigidity and less willing to adapt to a new schedule or perhaps a bit or a lot more aggressive on days preceding major cold fronts and during a full-moon cycle. I know that information may sound totally far-fetched, but it's something we noted back then and something that still rings true today.

While on its face the study was net neutral in terms of impact, which was disappointing for us, in addition to the revelations we learned during the journaling, another long-lasting benefit came out of it that was completely unexpected and unintended.

Taking part in the study required bloodwork from all of us–Lisa, Cameron, and me. We did not fill out lengthy paperwork on family history, but blood was a requirement. Aside from the painstaking task of getting a blood draw from Cameron, it was a fairly routine process I didn't think anything about. A couple of weeks later I had a missed call and voicemail from Dr. James asking me to give her a call. I didn't think anything about it, figuring she wanted to get an update on Cam. I was wrong.

Change You, Change Your World

After a few days of back and forth, I was finally able to connect with the doctor. She said she wanted to visit with me about the results of *my* bloodwork. Over the course of the conversation she told me my bloodwork had shown either markers or precursors (I cannot recall which actual phrase she used) for Alzheimer's and heart disease. Both possibilities wore heavily on me, but particularly the first. There was no way for the doctor to know that my grandmother had passed away eight years previous of Alzheimer's. As I mentioned, there was no family history information sought as part of the pre-work. As well, my dad had begun to show early signs of Alzheimer's. Although I didn't know it at the time, Dad would be diagnosed with early onset dementia/Alzheimer's in 2013 and pass away in fall of 2016.

Hearing this information from the doctor was unsettling at best, but I didn't make any significant life changes directly after that call. That would come a few months later.

People often chuckle when I tell them my personal

transformation story is twofold–I was lazy, and Oprah. The truth is, that's pretty much fact, though in the most interesting sequence of events imaginable and set against the backdrop of knowledge I had learned a few months prior from the doctor telling me what she had discovered in my bloodwork.

It was fall of 2006 and we were still in north central Arkansas. I was working a range of shifts, so I often had a weekday day off and a weekend day off. I can't remember what day of the week it was, but it was a weekday and I was off. The kids were at their respective schools and I was taking advantage of having time by myself at the house. I settled on the couch with my standbys: a can of coke and a bag of Cheetos.

Sometime over the course of channel surfing and munching I dozed off. When I woke up Oprah Winfrey was on, and as I reached for the remote to change it I heard her guest, Dr. Oz, being introduced. In front of him was a table full of organs. He was demonstrating the difference between a smoker and someone overweight to someone who wasn't. I'm not sure why it resonated with me on that day, as it certainly wasn't the first time in my life that I was introduced to the notion that my diet was not healthy. Heck, in five years going from a thirty-six waist to a forty-four waist and on the verge of upgrading again might have been hint number one; nonetheless, that day it hit me like a ton of bricks.

I had tried a lot of fad diets in the past and had indeed lost weight, only to gain it right back. In his conversation points that day, Dr. Oz actually mentioned that fact– that "going on a diet" is similar to holding your breath underwater. Eventually you have to come up for air, and in the diet world that meant going right back to your unhealthy habits. I decided that afternoon that it was time to get my life in order and start living healthier. It was time to engage in some type of cardio-based exercise daily and change my eating habits.

Changing the composition of my diet was quite radical and involved us completely changing everything in our pantry. Thankfully my wife, who was already a healthy person, agreed to take the journey with me. The rules were simple. Nothing with high fructose corn syrup, nothing with hydrogenated oils, nothing with enriched flour, and sugar or salt couldn't be in the first five ingredients. Last, I limited myself to one portion. I found that I always went back for a second helping simply because it tasted good, but not because I was hungry. While the rules of the game were simple, playing by the rules was not, especially in the first month. I had become addicted to a lifestyle full of sugary and starchy foods and drinks, but we made the change nonetheless, and eventually it became our lifestyle.

At the same time I took up running, though I use that term loosely, and also did sit ups and pushups. When I first started running I picked a route around the neighborhood that was 1.5 miles. Sadly, I couldn't run more than a quarter of a mile at a time and then walked until I caught my breath and then ran some more. I couldn't do more than fifteen sit ups and four pushups. It was a humbling start. I can't say that I know why, but I never gave up on it. A quarter of a mile at a time running turned into a half a mile, then one mile, then one and a half, and more. Fifteen sit ups became twenty, then twenty-five, fifty, seventy-five, and more. Four pushups became eight, twelve, twenty, thirty, and more. I was getting stronger and losing an incredible amount of weight. There were weeks that I would step on the scale and be seven pounds lighter. In three months I was back down to my "newly married" size of thirty-six waist and was running eighteen to twenty miles a week.

More than that, however, is that it improved everything around me. My new self-confidence resulted in happiness and contentment with myself, which resulted in a clearer and more focused mind to think through the situations in life. It is odd to admit it, but it was the first time that I focused on improving our situation as a family for the purpose of someone other than myself. Every decision I had made previous to those days was absolutely centered on me and driven by selfishness. Feeling better about me, because of a most unintended reason, resulted in the focus on everyone around me first.

It was spring of 2007, the year that Cameron would start kindergarten in the public school system in the fall. One day at work I received an email from the training and development division announcing a new approach to management training. Headquarters was looking for people who were interested in pursuing management as a career step. Although I wasn't sure what the position entailed, I was definitely a people person, and having been to many training classes for the company, I related to the role and decided to inquire a bit more. My wife and I discussed it lightly, but without having additional details we found it was very difficult to speak to the potential position with any definitiveness.

I got a prescreen call wherein I was able to ask a few questions and answer a few too. I learned the company was sourcing for three locations–Fayetteville, Arkansas; Springfield, Missouri; and Little Rock, Arkansas. Hearing the words Little Rock sent shivers down my spine, but the other two locations were foreign to us. If I was selected for an interview it would basically be for all three locations, and management would decide placement when narrowing down the candidate field, though individual preference would be considered.

I had learned from the sins of my past. I therefore made discussing this potential move with Lisa my priority number one. After a lengthy discussion, and assuring her we would *not* be moving back to Little Rock, regardless the offer, I decided to put in for the role. The school systems in Northwest Arkansas seemed to have some strong autism-specific programs, so that was definitely going to be my expressed focus. It was here that I would cross paths with Gene Tabor again. The Regional HR Manager who'd helped me all those years ago was now sitting across from me at the interview table. It truly is a small world. Thankfully the interview went well, and within a few weeks I received an official job offer for the Northwest Arkansas location.

I still remember the call I got on a Tuesday night informing me the company was extending the job offer to me. My feelings were mixed. Although we had made the decision as a family and felt like it would be a positive thing for our family, shades of relocations in the past weighed heavily on my mind. We were in a good place in Mountain Home. It had a great school system, though its autism-specific programs lagged significantly when contrasted with the larger and more well-funded school systems in Northwest Arkansas.

Both Lisa and I were happy, and things were as good as

they had ever been in our family. Was I about to mess things up with another relocation? I must have sounded reticent on the phone with the hiring manager, because she asked, "Aren't you excited?"

I played it off as being speechless I was so excited, but the truth was I knew a lot riding was riding on this change.

Embracing the New Normal

It has been a long time since we moved to Northwest Arkansas, and I can happily say without hesitation that outside of the decision to marry my wife, it was hands down the best decision I made. Of course, hindsight is always 20/20, isn't it?

Moving to Bentonville, Arkansas, looked good on paper and would play out to be a good decision, but we had some challenges in the early days that put red-flag warning signs up. We met the first challenge right away.

We relocated in April, which meant that Mya would have a whopping six weeks left of the school year. Although challenging for her to go to a new place, if there was a time to do it, it was when she was in the first grade, when everyone is friends and it's kind of cool being the new kid. It did reveal one of the biggest parenting-fail moments of our young parenting experience, though. Mya's birthday is the first week of June, and with her being new to the area, we weren't sure how to go about throwing her a party.

We invited family, as usual, but logistical challenges

prevented most from making the three-hour trek, and Lisa's parents were the only ones who committed to coming over. In a stroke of genius, we decided that since we didn't know anyone in her class, we would simply invite *everyone*, hoping a handful of kids would turn out. We requested an RSVP so we would have some idea of what to expect. As the days leading to her party dwindled and we didn't hear from anyone, we weren't sure what to expect.

Erring on the extreme side of caution we decided to buy plenty, assuming people would show up without RSVPing. A quick trip to Sam's Club did the trick, and we had more than plenty in the event that we had a houseful of kids and parents show up. The magical day approached, and we put the piñata in the backyard, balloons on the mailbox, and streamers in the house. And then we waited, us in the living room and Mya looking out the window of her room. And we waited and waited and waited. No one showed. It was becoming clear that we had made a big mistake and set Mya up for disappointment. In typical Mya fashion she never let it show, though as parents we knew it had to be tough on her.

In reflection of the years before and since that event it's certainly made me realize what a special girl we have in Mya. Siblings of those with autism have to endure quite a bit, and at least in her case, they must mature and grow up much quicker. Cameron demands most of the attention in the household by default. Our lives are centered on his schedule and routine, and there is impact to Mya as well. What is incredibly impressive is how she handles it in stride and has become the biggest champion for her brother. She advocates for special-needs kids often, a direct result of growing up exposed to autism. One time she had to give a presentation on any topic of her choosing at school. She chose to address the casual use of the *R* word (retarded) and how it had no place as a joke or insult. She has always been well beyond her years in maturity.

The timing of the move to Bentonville posed service-based challenges for Cameron. In Mountain Home he had attended a preschool serving kids with special needs, and he also received his therapies. What we failed to investigate a bit further was placement and services for Cameron in the gap leading up to August when school started and he would be in kindergarten. It was only after moving we realized the full list of most providers. While it's commonplace for us now, we still had not learned to filter everything, every single decision, through a how-will-this-impact-Cameron filter. Nowadays it is our second nature to consider the impact on Cameron before we approach any major event.

The only misstep in the relocation was exclusive to its timing. While we were excited for Cameron to start school, the abrupt halt to the routine and schedule he had grown accustomed to and the services he was being provided created some behavioral concerns we realized immediately. The old doubts crept in as tension in the Leachman household ran high. Cameron was five years old and still not potty-trained. He still demanded much of the time in the house, as he was highly prone to putting himself at risk.

We soon learned the challenges of having a child with the size and strength of a five-year-old yet the curiosity, social awareness, and understanding of risk to self of a toddler, which is absolutely no awareness. Three events stand out in my mind as the starkest examples. The first was a trip that he and Lisa took to Walmart to get groceries. Cameron was becoming more capable of handling the stimulus-rich environment of a large shopping center with a large amount of activity that once was a source of great angst for him. In fact, he was growing fond of the experience and seemed to approach it with a sense of adventure.

His favorite parts of the store were the produce department, because of his love for navel oranges, and of course, the toy department. During this particular trip something did not sit well with Cam. He had grown too big to sit in the shopping basket. Typically holding his hand while walking through the store was not an issue, but not on that day. He became upset and fought Lisa, trying to free himself. He pulled his body weight to the floor and yelled in Spanish, thanks to Dora the Explorer, *"Ayudame! Ayudame!"* Help me, help me, at the top of his lungs. It was a challenging experience for Lisa to endure. She called me later that afternoon very upset, to the point of tears.

A couple of times Cameron also revealed his capabilities as an escape artist, especially when we have not paid attention to detail. It was very easy to be lulled into a sense of security with Cameron and let your edge down. We had decorated the house for fall with a small scarecrow in the flower garden in the front of the house. Cameron absolutely loved that little figure. He was fascinated with the scarecrow's nose and grabbed it often when he was on the way inside the house.

One day when he grabbed the nose and it fell off, which upset Cameron. We let him keep the nose, which quickly became torn and tattered. We discarded it without his knowledge. We thought all had been forgotten, but little did we know that Cameron was devising a master plan. One day we were inside the house while Cameron played on the swing set in the backyard. We had the door open so we could keep a close eye on him, but we got distracted momentarily. A glance in the backyard a few minutes later revealed no Cameron. I assumed he'd gone over to the side of house to play with the hose, so I causally made my way out back and to the side. There was no Cameron. With a higher sense of urgency, I made my way to the other side of the house where the gate was located. To my horror I found the gate was open. I ran out and looked both ways, only to see Cameron in the middle of the street. He was running back *toward* the house holding something orange. Our neighbor five houses down had erected a similar scarecrow whose nose was still intact, and sometime during commutes to town and back, Cameron had taken notice. Envisioning him running in the middle of the road–though a neighborhood street–still gives me chills today. It was the first time we became aware of the level of intelligence that lay beneath the surface with Cameron.

If the previous example gave me chills, the next experience was enough to shake the entire family to our core. It stands as a stark reminder that the environment within which you live is unexplainable and hard to transfer to other environments. We live a life of 'lockdown' with multiple locks on every door where potential danger to Cameron exists on the other side. It's our normal environment, that to another seems excessive.

One weekend we made the three-hour trip to Little Rock to spend time with Lisa's parents. As was often the case when we went down there, Lisa and I took the opportunity to have a few moments to ourselves. Parenting a high-need child creates a struggle with finding childcare that one can trust. The result created limited opportunities for us to have a date. It was always nice, and it still is today, when we get those moments to ourselves, whether just a few hours or perhaps a weekend getaway. While I do not recall the specifics of where Lisa and I went for a couple hours, I will never forget our arrival back at her parents' house.

As we pulled into the driveway her dad was outside on the front porch, which was not uncommon, but we could tell that he was visibly shaken. After we went inside we found the rest of the family: Lisa's mom, Mya, and Cameron. However, Lisa's mom was emotional, as was Mya. We learned that while they were in the house busy tending to other things, Cameron slipped out the front door and into the backyard. It was fall, and through the bare trees, a playground at a nearby school was visible. It typically was not visible from that house, because of the tree foliage.

The problem was there was a very steep hill and an extremely busy street to cross if taking a direct route to the park from their house. That route was precisely Cameron's plan. When the family discovered Cameron's absence—notable by the open front door—everyone made a mad scramble to find him. I can only imagine the impending feeling of doom as they searched the house frantically, trying to come to grips with where he went. A glimpse into the backyard revealed nothing, as Cameron had already descended below the line of sight.

Thankfully Lisa's dad didn't waste any time in broadening

the search. He jumped in his truck and exited the neighborhood, a route that would take him by the park. When he pulled out, he saw Cameron on the sidewalk. Two adults had him occupied. He got out and spoke to the couple and discovered it was an off-duty police officer and a social worker, a couple, who had been driving when they came upon Cameron and realized that something was not right. He was standing on the side of the road covering his ears. They intervened, most likely mitigating a potentially tragic situation.

Being an Autism Dad

Life with Cameron has been a consistent experience of read, respond, and react. It is next to impossible to predict the things he might do as a result of his proneness to explore coupled with his lack of sense of danger. No one warns you of those things, and the price of discovery is accompanied by a lot of risk.

Cameron's escape from home and attempt to reach the park on his own prompted the first of many modifications inside the Leachman household. We started with child-protective door handles, which he eventually was able to over-power. We transitioned to clasp locks near the top of the door, which he eventually learned to pull a chair to, climb onto the chair, and unlock. We then transitioned to double-keyed deadbolts, so that exiting the house required a key the same as entering the house. Out of fear that one night we might leave a key on the counter or he would discover our hiding spot, we ultimately landed on a house alarm. I tell people all the time that most people have an alarm to keep people out, while we have an alarm centered on keeping one person in.

If there is one decision I wish we could get a mulligan for, it would be the decision to waive a year of school during his kindergarten through fourth-grade time. You know what they say, hindsight is 20/20, and that decision is definitely one I wish we could take back. The state of Arkansas allows parents to require their child to repeat a grade. We decided it would be best to do so in the early education years, especially given the rate of progress he was making with his time at Bentonville in its autism classroom. His first K-4 teacher was awesome, and we hoped to extend his time in that setting under her tutelage. What we discovered later was that in his early childhood years—specifically the third- and fourth-grade times—we ultimately stymied his progress for a brief period.

As a five-year third grader and a six-year fourth grader, Cameron became one of the least needy in the room. Imagine having an autism classroom consisting of kindergarten through fourth grade, where all grades are in one room. The chasm between needs and abilities in that grade range was quite substantial. In reflection we sure would like to still have that card in our back pocket today and have him repeat time in either junior high or high school, when the playing field is more level with abilities across the age group in the class. I strongly advise anyone with the ability to waive a year to do it, but do so with a lot of thought put into the timing.

One thing that we have realized throughout Cameron's transitions is that we typically lose progress the first year of any transition between school programs. As a larger school district, Bentonville has a few transitions: kindergarten through fourth, middle school, junior high, and high school.

In reflection each "first" has been accompanied with behavior challenges and a bit of a plateau of growth. I wish the school could figure out how to remove one or two of those transitions, at least for the higher-need kiddos.

Similar to the transition challenges within the first year of a new program, we often saw Cameron struggle with the transitions within the year as well. He does well when multiple weeks of a similar routine are stretched together. Where he struggles is when there are hiccups in his established routine, such as the beginning or end to breaks for spring, summer, Thanksgiving, and Christmas. Each disruption to the routine is accompanied by a new relearning phase where the new routine is embraced, even if it is the same as it was the previous year.

During disrupted routines we often see Cameron have what we call the delayed onset of resistance. Life can pretty much be clicking along normally in the first few days of a new transition and then suddenly, seemingly out of the blue, we see behavior indicative of a transition challenge, coupled with a high degree of emotional outbursts; a more restrictive, rigid need; and often aggressive behavior.

It's odd that things such as transitional challenges, or the way of life in raising a child on the spectrum (or I'm sure any high-need child), creates a home environment that is completely familiar to the immediate family but completely foreign to others. To ward off any dangers or meltdowns it might take changes to your physical environment – like the double-keyed deadbolts and alarm system. But schedules are a real thing in the Leachman home. There are times Cameron can live in a less structured, weekly or monthly schedule, but there are also times that we need to write out and specific scheduled tasks by day around critical timeframes. We see this become a need during times of transition, breaks in school, significant changes in the established routine, etc.

As an example, Cameron has established that he must have his 1:30 p. m. snack, 6:00 bath on Wednesday nights, 6:30 snack, and 8:30 "bedtime" (in quotes because he wants only to go through the motions of going to bed, such as prayers, brushing his teeth, etc., but subsequently gets up and walks around the house for about an hour and a half). These things are so routine for us that we don't even think through them, we just do them. Yet when we are exposed to the looseness of others' routines, or when they are plunged into the structure of ours, we realize quite fully the rigidity within which we live.

When Lisa and I do have the opportunity to go out, Lisa spends hours beforehand scripting copious notes and play-by-plays of critical information related to Cam's schedule to help her mom or mine navigate our very scripted life with ease. Cameron will nearly always test the waters when mom and dad are away. His favorite trick is to try to sneak an extra snack in or ask to be in my office where he knows the Xbox and PlayStation are. Lisa's diary of notes helps not only inform others of his routine, but also keep Cam from getting into things he isn't supposed to be in.

Magical Moments

I mentioned earlier in this book that I don't believe in fate or chance. Moments in life and chance encounters orchestrated by God create magical moments in life that change the trajectory for a person, and we experienced two such moments during Cameron's junior high days. They were life altering for both Cameron and me.

The first was a run-of-the-mill IEP meeting. For those of you who have endured these federally mandated Individualized Education Program meetings for children with special needs, you know what I mean. The formality of sitting around a table annually and signing papers can be mundane. Granted, there are times one needs to be assertive and "grab the bull by the horns" in these meetings. Stay tuned; I'll give an example later. However, when there is a basis of trust established with a school, teacher, and parent, though, those meetings can seem somewhat routine. The vast majority of our IEP meetings fall into this category. Good conversation followed by the grand signing ceremony. This particular meeting, however,

Cameron's physical education teacher was present, and he referred to Cameron's enjoyment of a particular line drill the teacher ran in the gym. Not only did Cameron seem to enjoy it, but he also outperformed his peer group, composed of the general education population. I made a mental note of how cool that fact was, but hadn't quite made the connection full connection yet.

A few months later Cameron and I were taking one our once-a-month trips to Cabelas, a sporting goods store. Cameron has a monthly calendar hanging on his wall where activities are posted. We did four things once a month, and he decided on which Saturday each would be done. Here are the four things:

A trip to Walmart. We have taken these trips since Cameron was five years old. He gets to pick out something small but meaningful to him. It used to be all about the color orange, so he would pick navel oranges or mini pumpkins, when in season. We have transitioned these trips into life skills trips now. We try to help Cameron understand budget and price by giving him a certain amount and letting him search for things within that budget. He is 18 today and we still have a long way to go for him to grasp this, but are confident he will.

A trip to The Home Depot. Cameron calls it 'Orange Store'. Are you picking up on his passion for the color orange? This trip consisted of nothing other than a walk around the store. Cameron wanted to explore some aisles more than others, but generally it was just a fifteen-to-twenty-minute journey walking around the store and getting an orange soda from the coolers near the checkouts on our way out.

A trip to Cabela's (now Bass Pro). Okay, I'll admit it; I had a lot to do with starting this ritual, but Cameron loves seeing the animals around the store and I loved checking out the latest archery equipment. As it turns out the animals and the aquarium were right next to the archery department; the perfect coincidence!

A meal in a restaurant. Follow me here: we were very selective with where we chose and helped steer Cameron towards an acceptable venue. It was typically a fast-food establishment or similar. Cameron's capability to hold his own in a quieter environment was low, so we were careful where we went for the

For about six months every time we went to Cabela's, Cameron pointed across the street to a restaurant called Houlihan's and said, "Dinner, Houlihan's?" It was Cameron's unique way of asking a question in a mind-ninja kind of way. He said something he wanted repeated to him so that he could reply his emphatic "Yes!"

I always dissuaded him from Houlihan's and turn his attention back to Cabela's. We had no desire to thrust ourselves into the environment at Houlihan's. Houlihan's was a little calmer, classier environment than we thought Cam could handle, and we tried to be sensitive to both his experience as well as that of the other patrons of the restaurant.

I never knew what Cameron's obsession with Houlihan's was, let alone how he knew it was a restaurant. It wouldn't be until several months later we learned that Cameron's way of looking up something or somewhere he was interested in was Googling it on his iPhone. Cameron had a phone for games and such, but once we discovered his Google activity, it opened up to us the world of a kid with limited vocabulary.

It became a literal treasure trove of nuggets about what was on Cameron's mind, and we have used it consistently since. When Cameron is not feeling well, he will search terms like "ouch throat" or "ouch head." For birthdays and Christmases, we can see what kind of toys he has been searching. We have learned that when we are going on trips, he Googles the destination and goes to street-level views to get a feel of the environment. And there, tucked deep into the browsing history, was Houlihan's, along with a full review of its menu and interior pics.

One Saturday, therefore, I decided to give in. Cameron's months-long, maximum-pressure campaign succeeded. I yielded to the pleading and consistent pressure after six months and decided it was time to let Cameron scratch the itch he'd been asking for. The response to his question, "Dinner, Houlihan's?" and my reciprocal, "Do you want dinner at Houlihan's?" was met with a YES! for the first time and a huge ear-to-ear grin. I called Lisa and let her know. We decided it would be best to go around four in the afternoon, so we could slide between the late lunch crowd and the dinner crowd and have a calmer environment for him.

A Life-Changing Dinner

We made the right choice of when to visit Houlihan's. The restaurant might have had three customers in it at the time we started, but it was beginning to fill up by the time we left. We will always look back fondly on our experience that day. First, the booth seats are out-of-this-world incredible. If you have ever wondered where the moon shoes of the 1980s went, I am convinced Houlihan's repurposed them into booth seats.

Cameron picked up quickly that if he bounced on his end, it thrust me up, and then we'd seesaw back and forth. Aside from the comfort and versatility of the booths, the service was second to none. When you have a kiddo like Cam, you know there are going to be moments in public that are either awesome or awkward. As Cameron was well in his teens at this point, it only takes a few seconds of interaction with Cameron to realize he isn't a typical teenage child, and that afternoon was no different.

As my wife ordered an orange soda for him and asked for it in a to-go cup with a top, because of the tendency of regular glasses to get spilled, our server, Morgan, acted as if it was no big deal. When we ordered and I asked that his chicken tenders be put outside the heat lamp for a few minutes before serving, because Cameron doesn't wait for his food to cool before he dives in, my special request was again met with a "No problem!" You'd be surprised how many times requests like this were met with resistance from other establishments.

Morgan engaged with Cameron on his level each time she came to the table. I could tell she knew, and it didn't matter. It was a cool experience. Later that evening I created a Facebook post and tagged Houlihan's in it. It was simple, explaining how grateful we were that we chose to eat there and the pleasant experience the staff gave Cameron. That was it, or so I thought.

I had a message in my inbox a couple days later from the restaurant that dropped my jaw. It basically read something like this: "Hi, John! We were so glad to see that you and your family had a good time at our restaurant the other night. We understand that routine is very important for kids with autism and just wanted to reach out to say if you ever know when you are coming back, we'd love to replicate the experience." I was shocked when I read it. As luck would have it, we had already put the April calendar together, and you guessed it, Cameron wanted to go back to Houlihan's on the third Saturday of the month.

I replied to the manager, letting her know when we'd be there and about the same time.

I was shocked when I read the first Facebook message from the manager, but I was completely dumbfounded the day we were going to eat there again. As we approached the front doors, Morgan opened the doors for us and greeted Cameron. She took us back to the same booth where we'd eaten before, where his orange drink in a to-go cup was already waiting. She said, "Are you having the chicken tenders tonight?" To which his response was an emphatic yes. It was another awesome experience, and it wasn't over. At the end of the night the head chef came out with the gift of an apron and a hat. Every member of the staff had signed Cameron's apron and put some message on it. It was a cool experience.

We thought that was it, but we were wrong. When we went home that night, we put Cam's apron up in his closet, not thinking anything more about it, but clearly Cameron was thinking about it. Cam's favorite show then and now is *SpongeBob*, and SpongeBob's profession is a cook. Something sparked Cam's imagination with that apron, we believe, as he linked it to his favorite show. The next morning, he came out of the room with his apron on and helped his mom cook his breakfast. He had been a kid that always waited for breakfast, his entire life, but now he was participating in it. To this day Cameron helps Lisa with meals, dinner preparation, and such.

As I watched him that morning it hit me that up to that point I had defined Cameron by what he couldn't do. I had looked at his limits first, and in doing so, had limited his abilities. I instantly reflected back to several months prior and the discussion we'd had in his IEP meeting about his enthusiasm and ability in the physical education drills. Watching him cooking breakfast that morning I asked myself, might he enjoy running? I had been running since 2007. I wondered if he would enjoy running with me.

I pondered this question for a couple weeks and asked

him one day if he wanted to go for a run. His answer was a yes, though I didn't know if he was really into it. We ran together for a half mile, and then back a half mile. He gave me absolutely no indication that he enjoyed it and simply went about his day. I wouldn't know until the next day when I came home from lunch that he had loved it. When I walked in the door he was there to greet me. He said, "You want running?" This was Cameron's way of getting me to ask him a question.

I repeated the phrase, "Cameron, you want running?"

The response was "Yes!" Obviously he was looking forward to the run and had enjoyed it.

Our journey continued like that for the next month or so. We never went more than a half mile out and then a half mile back, each day at lunch. It was a contained route within a quiet neighborhood, since I was worried about his safety. He required constant oversight, because he was not aware of how to stay on the correct side of the road for traffic or that he had to stop at stop signs and look both ways.

His love for running was obvious every time we went out, which made me wonder if he could participate in cross-country running at school. He was about to transition to junior high, where it would be possible for him to participate in such a sport. I requested a meeting to discuss it with the school.

Remember earlier when I mentioned there are times you have to "take the bull by the horns" in some meetings? Yeah, this meeting was definitely one of those times.

It became clear to me that the cross-country coach was not overly supportive of Cameron's joining the team and that was clear from the beginning. Some of the comments she made at the meeting enraged me because of the tone. At one point I simply stopped the meeting, looked at the principal, and said, "He *will* be running cross-country next year. I will make myself available to be his guide on practices as we acclimate him. I need you to have a conversation with your head coach and make sure the mindset is correct. How she chooses to interact with and include Cameron in front of his peer group will go a long way in his acceptance on the team and a life lesson for all of them."

The principal understood. It was obvious the only person at the meeting that morning averse to Cam running was the coach, and the rest of the IEP team was embarrassed at the approach she had taken. We agreed that I would get our son ready over the summer and help with his integration into the team.

It Takes a Community

I have to say, Bentonville, Arkansas, is a special place. When I posted on Facebook about Cameron's passion for running and that I was beginning some preparation work to get him ready for cross-country, the responses were overwhelming. We then landed on an official date in late June and created a Facebook event for it.

Someone posted that we should get shirts made up with the phrase "You Want Running?" Quickly, one of the runners, a good friend of mine who was a graphic designer, had the absolute perfect design: the phrase centered on the shirt with two sets of shoe prints surrounding it, one size larger than the other, to depict a dad and son's journey.

I reached out to Mike Rush, the owner of a local running store called Rush Running, to inquire who to use for getting shirts printed. When I explained the situation and what we were doing, he offered to bring his big inflatable start/finish line to the event for Cameron. Although I didn't know it at the time, Mike also coordinated to pay for the shirts for the run, and we ended up having just short of fifty people show up.

Imagine that! Fifty people, some who didn't know Cameron, showed up to support him for a two-mile journey. They ran beside and behind him the entire time, letting him set the pace and cross the finish line first. It was truly special.

What I saw in Cameron prior to the start and during that run was something unique. In his everyday environment prior to that day Cameron preferred to be away from the crowd, if not absolutely avoiding large groups of people altogether. It was completely opposite on that day. That day he thrived on the pre-race environment. Music was playing and there was the usual hustle and bustle of a crowd of folks getting ready to run. I could see the enjoyment on Cameron's face as he soaked in the environment, almost as if he was stepping outside himself and setting autism on the shelf. That behavior is the same today. He thoroughly enjoys the pre-race environment, and the bigger the better.

For the rest of the summer he continued to run with me four or five days a week, anywhere from two to three miles. He named the routes based on different things we passed. One of his favorites was the "little Walmart" route. This one took us to a Walmart Neighborhood Market where we turned around to come back. What he loved about this route was the stoplight crosswalks. He *loves* pressing buttons and hearing them beep. He doesn't quite understand the goal of pressing the button in the direction you intend to head; he just presses them both in excess until the light is favorable in our direction. Sadly, this behavior has resulted in a few drivers getting upset with him for causing a red light for no apparent reason since we don't always cross the side of the street for the button he's pressed. We've had our fair share of glares and the occasional one-finger salutes, but he unapologetically continues. And I unapologetically allow it (insert smile here).

Cameron sporting his new "You want running" shirt

Cameron under the Rush Running finish marker

Cameron's first group run

Cam's cross-country running journey was a special time in his life. We were nervous about the experience, wondering how the team would react to him. Our worries quickly subsided. The coach and I had a meeting on day one and she apologized for the earlier approach. She was genuinely interested in Cameron and excited to see him develop. The bond created amid a team environment was awesome to watch develop. I made myself available to the school for his morning practice. I felt it was important to acclimate Cam to the team slowly as well as acclimate the team to him. I had also learned of Cam's inability to interpret danger and feared there might be a tendency to overestimate his ability to care for himself during routes that required waiting for traffic and crossing the road.

In the early days the team wasn't sure how to take Cameron. He has tics and marches to the beat of his own drum. His happy humming and other noises he makes during stretches and runs were met with perplexed looks. Don't get me wrong; none of the kids were mean, they were just trying to figure out this new kid.

Two moments stood out during that first year. One morning some thunderstorms were rolling in, so the coach moved the practice indoors, in the gym. Since it was indoors team members opted to run drills, since distance running wasn't going to be possible. I sat on the bleachers and watched. During one of the drills it was obvious to me that Cameron was having a bit of a struggle picking up the intent and what to do. Every part of me wanted to run out on the floor before it was his turn to lead, but I sat back, and I am glad I did. One of the popular girls, Rachel, saw Cam wasn't quite grasping it and ran back to help him. It was a "larger than the moment" moment. The rest of the team saw her helping him, and from that point on there was a "we've got his back" approach.

I'll never forget the meet that following Saturday. Prior to that day I would line up behind Cameron in the starting chute. He wanted me to be there. I think it provided him a bit of calm. That Saturday, however, three of the boys on the team gently guided him into the fold and talked quietly to him, giving him high fives and subtle hands on his shoulder during the pre-race. If there was any doubt before, he was definitely an adopted member of the Timberwolf tribe from that day on.

As mentioned earlier, transitions have always been disruptors in Cameron's life, and we decided to pull him out of cross-country during the transition from junior high to high school. The school was willing to explore and support his continuation in cross-country, but one of the things I learned the first year of Cameron's running was how he did it for himself, not for others. His approach to running actually kind of changed my outlook toward it. He's completely noncompetitive. That's not to say he isn't fast or strong, it's just a description of his approach to running. Time is not important to him; beating someone is not important to him. You don't see him go into an all-out sprint when the finish line is in sight. He is simply to content to run at whatever pace he's feeling in the moment, which is why Lisa and I thought that high school cross-country might be a bit of a stretch for him. The runners get super competitive at that age, aside from the fact that the transition to a new school, new teachers, a new routine and bell schedule, etc., would be hard enough to navigate.

Running remains a central part of Cameron's life. It is hard to describe his joy for running, but it was clear we he wanted to continue the morning routine of running. I decided to enroll him in a half-marathon training program the community puts on in advance of the annual Bentonville Half Marathon, the best half marathon anyone will ever experience. I had run it for a few years and wondered how Cam would take to longer distance running. If he didn't like it, that was fine, but I had a "nothing ventured, nothing gained" approach to everything with Cam, and at a minimum, it was worth exploring.

The half-marathon training group met every Saturday morning at seven o'clock. Week one started out with a one-mile run, and it built up to twelve miles a couple weeks prior to the actual half marathon. It would be the perfect opportunity to place him in an environment he loved–two hundred people meeting every Saturday to conquer the pavement. Just like his passion for running was clear from day one, so was his love for distance running. He gobbled up the increased distances without a problem and looked forward to the Saturday morning training sessions.

His first half marathon was an awesome experience. I'll never forget all of the "Go Cam!" screaming I heard throughout the course. The running community had wrapped its arms around Cameron, embraced him, and rallied behind him. Watching him finish and get that big medal around his neck was a special moment.

I meet him on his terms; he brings me into his world. Even though he has a limited vocabulary, we have brief engagements on every run. Maybe it's pointing to and saying "squirrel", or when he says "roots" as we cross the low water bridge that has some erosion along the creek side.

His favorite running activity is to spell words and ask me what it spells. A few of his favorites go something like this: "E-l-e-p-h-a-n-t, what's spell, Dad?" (he always leaves out the word 'that' when asking what something spells) to which I reply, "Elephant," and he will say, "Elephant trumpet, Dad," expecting me to mimic an elephant. I do my best. I'm sure people we are passing are wondering why I am trumpeting like an elephant, chattering like a monkey, mooing like a cow, neighing like a horse, crowing like a rooster, or panting like a puppy, but it's all worth it. My only wish is that he'd learn to do these things only on flats or downhills. Unfortunately for me he loves to do it when we are going up a hill! ☺

Our running journey is three years young at this point. As of April 4, 2020, he's completed ten half marathons, a 25K, and too many 5Ks and 10Ks to mention. Five o'clock morning training runs in the rain, sleet, snow, heat, or humidity are commonplace for him. Cameron and I have run just shy of two thousand miles together. I have a hashtag that I use for nearly every post I do with Cameron and his runs: #EveryMileaMemory

Each mile we run strengthens a bond I never thought would exist. I thought, back in 2006, that I was changing my life for me. That losing the weight, stopping the smoking, and beginning a healthier lifestyle of exercise was about me. While that was definitely the way it started, I had no idea that years later it would be the activity that creates a best-friend relationship with my son.

Cameron enjoying a daily run

Thumbs Up, dad!

One of Cameron's favorite country routes

The Ups and Downs of Autism

The mid and late teenage years proved to be difficult for Cameron to navigate. Up to that point life had been on a fairly steady state of cruise control. I'll go back to something referenced earlier: transitions are extremely difficult for kiddos like Cameron to navigate. Now, consider that some schools require a transition from elementary to middle school and then a transition from middle school to junior high, and yet another transition from junior high to high school. Add to that the raging hormones that all kids go through in their teens, another difficult thing for kid like Cam, and you set the stage for the daily tinderbox of emotions we encountered during that time.

Around the age of sixteen Cameron started having significant behavior issues with what can only be best described as spontaneous combustion. The day could be going along fine, and it would take one minor incident to rapidly escalate into aggressive outbursts with physical pushing, kicking, and hitting toward those around him. Calls from the school were becoming an all-too-familiar occurrence. It wasn't just happening at school, either. Cameron had the same outbursts at home. Most of the time they occurred when I was on the road for work. The helplessness I felt on the other end of the phone line while sitting in a hotel nine hundred miles away was difficult, but not nearly as difficult a time as my wife was having.

Let me give credit to someone who deserves much more than I could ever give her: my wife, Lisa. There is no way to describe the things she has dealt with over the course of Cameron's eighteen years while I have been at work. Unless you live it, you wouldn't know how restrictive a life is when you have a high-need child. Lisa has been and remains the absolute rock of our family.

As we navigated this time in Cameron's life, we were clueless as the root of the issues. We threw virtually every tool in our toolbox at it, from schedule review and increased rigor/structure in his day-to-day, to reward systems, all of which fell flat in terms of response. For the first time in our life we were going to explore something we had avoided Cam's entire life: medication.

Cam's doctor had made passive recommendations in the past about considering medication, but we wanted none of it. Our concern was we would significantly alter who Cameron was. Yes, the excessive tantrums and aggression toward self and others were difficult to endure, but we calculated it comprised less than 10 percent of a given week's behavior. Why alter him all the time for something that was such a small part of his life? The conversations with the doctor became more transparent as Cameron's behavior intensified. The spontaneous combustion moments were becoming more intense.

Cameron's rigidity in approaching his day and environment was also increasing during this time. Whereas once we could make subtle changes to his day, he had severe reactions and ramifications to minor changes now. He became insistent about Lisa's appearance, wanting her hair up in ponytails and deciding which evening robe she could wear, etc. At one doctor visit I said it was like Cameron was tightening his grip on every part of his life and environment, and every time we yielded a little bit, his behavior just got worse.

The doctor's response resonated with us at last. "I know you want to avoid medication, but when it gets to the point where quality of life is impacted for either you or him or both, it's time to consider it."

After avoiding the conversation for twelve years post diagnosis, we reluctantly agreed to begin a low-dose regimen of Sertraline to attempt putting Cameron at ease.

Even with years of autism behind us, we still learn something new every day and with every experience we go through. Although several years prior, when Cameron was a small child, I had done some journaling of behavior and days, it was a practice we had fallen out of the habit of doing consistently. Journaling, even with the smallest notation of observations, helps a great deal. It is something I highly recommend parents do. It makes evaluating the impact of decisions made, such as medication, easier to evaluate after several weeks, since none of us can remember subtle changes over the course of time. It is incredibly helpful to look back at data one has collected vs. trying to remember it all (and failing).

When Cameron was younger, I wasn't necessarily looking to find or prove anything when I journaled. At that time, I was just trying to understand autism. Over the course of time I discovered the significant impact the full moon cycle–usually one day prior and one day after–and the day before a strong cold front had on his behavior. It has remained consistent throughout time and is still the case today. We know to expect more rigidity in routine from Cameron on those days and the increased likelihood of an outburst, as he has an on-edge behavior style. Our knowledge gained from journaling helps us know how to engage with Cameron and proactively mitigate behaviors during typically more difficult times. It's helped us prep new teachers throughout Cameron's life, so they know what to expect and create action plans in the classroom and during transitions in anticipated trouble times. Keep a journal! Regardless of how insignificant the behavior you write down may seem, you may be surprised what you discover when looking at it over the course of several weeks and months.

Despite the good things that came from our journaling early in Cam's life, we are human and forgot to do it during our major decision to begin the Sertraline. The result was confusion several months later, when we asked ourselves whether it was working. The behavior was still present, but we hadn't done a great job at being able to definitively say whether it was improving, staying the same, or getting worse.

The onset of the time we started Cameron on Sertraline for severe aggression collided with another major change in our life. I was recruited by Target as they were going through a renewed effort to revitalize its focus in the food side of the retail business. The role was a terrific opportunity to expand the breadth and depth of my retail experience, specifically in food, to a large group in the Midwest. It also meant a relocation to Olathe, Kansas, about three and a half hours north of where we were living in Northwest Arkansas. After discussing the pros and cons, we decided that the opportunity was right for us to pursue, and in the summer of 2018, we found ourselves residents of Kansas. I had accepted the role earlier in the year and commuted back and forth for four months while Cameron finished his ninth-grade year and Mya finished her senior year. We relocated as a family in June.

The move to Olathe was both great and horrible at the same time. We were very impressed with Cameron's school. Olathe West High School (Go Owls!) will always have a special place in our heart. When I say the faculty embraced Cameron, it doesn't even come close to describing how much every person he interacted with at Olathe West invested in him. I had never seen such a complete and holistic approach to his educational experience and his future as we experienced in Olathe. It's not uncommon to find individuals in the education experience who go all in with it, but at Olathe West, the entire team, literally everyone who interacted with Cameron, cared deeply about his success as a student.

To that end it brings to light why the experience was so challenging. We were a party to the awesomeness of the Olathe West team, because of the challenges we went through with Cameron while there. I think now it was naive for us to expect Cameron to make the transition without challenges. It was a difficult time in his life. The teenage years are challenging enough for anyone. Raging hormones and growth spurts are hard enough to go through. Add autism to that mix, and you have a tinder box nearly daily.

We were encountering some challenges with his behavior

prior to moving, so it makes sense the behavior issues would continue, but we were caught off guard by Cameron's initial reaction to relocation. It was as if he didn't miss a beat. We were intentional with the home we bought, trying to mirror the home that we rent for vacation in Florida each year. We found a multi-level home that gave everyone their own living space. Clearly Cameron was headed into adulthood, and since he will always be under our roof as a dependent adult, we wanted to approach it from a buy-for-the-future standpoint. At first things went smoothly. Almost too smoothly, we thought, and we were right.

From June until late fall life was blissful. Cameron stacked good days on top of good days, with only a few exceptions of the occasional outburst. We were exploring the new parts of Kansas City, all the barbeque options and fun things to do. We tried out new donut shops on Sunday mornings, a tradition Cam and I started during junior high. He loves the three chocolate-with-sprinkles donuts he gets every Sunday morning, as long as he has a good week with no outbursts or aggression.

Little did we know what lurked around the corner. In late fall/early winter, things started to unwind rapidly with Cameron. We started seeing a sharp increase of intense OCD in him and an uptick in aggressive behavior with those around him. The behavior intensified after the turn of the new year. We had returned home for Christmas break to visit family and trying to transition him back into school and back in the groove after the break did not go well. Severe outbursts and unacceptable behavior that was once the exception was becoming the rule.

The aggressive behavior demonstrated toward teachers

and family was difficult to digest. At the same time, he un-explainably stopped sitting down and also stopped going to his room during the day. His room had always been his es-cape and a place that brought him comfort. Now he stood at the edge of the kitchen table or counter all day and wanted to control the environment–what was on TV, what Alexa was playing, etc. Our once nimble, flexible son was becoming increasingly rigid and controlling. In many ways it felt like we were prisoners in our own home. We were lost.

I will never forget the morning that I went to wake him up for our morning run, which was something we had done for a couple years at that point. It was hard coded into his routine. More importantly, it was something he enjoyed, like an outlet for him. But not that morning. He uttered, "No running."

I was taken aback. I tried to talk him into it, knowing how much he enjoyed the activity and thinking maybe he was a bit tired, but it was obvious from his adamant approach that he was not going to run that day. Then there were many more days like that one. It hit my soul hard. Truth be told, though I had loved running since I started several years prior, the best part of my day was the run with Cam. I loved it because of the relationship we were building and the 'talks' we had. That first solo run around what was once his favorite loop in Olathe, Kansas, was lonely. I didn't like it. I wanted my son back.

I altered my approach with him and began to run a little later in the day and over the weekend, but I left him alone for the early morning events to let him sleep. Even the runs he took were different. I could see the conflict he was dealing with. He *wanted* to run, but at the same time it was as if he didn't. He was having an internal battle of desiring to do something yet having anguish about it. He joined me occasionally, and I always kept it upbeat so he could enjoy something from it or have something to look forward to. He still craved the race environment but was struggling with the approach to day-to-day training to be prepared for such an event.

Lisa and I were always trying to strike a delicate balance. To what degree do we live our life versus being accommodating to Cameron's sensitivities and OCD. To what degree should we give in when he made increasing demands for changes in routine, or do we continue to live our life and just help bring him along? Finding what your child is *capable* of doing as opposed to *incapable of tolerating* is much more challenging to discover than it sounds. We tried everything to address the issue and could never come to a good result.

Aggression and excessive fits of rage were commonplace. His size and strength made this very difficult to endure, especially when I was out of the house. He has a very considerable size advantage over Lisa and Mya. Out of an abundance of caution, we actually pulled him from school for the final few weeks after a major incident resulted in injury to teachers or aides. I do have to say that the school was most helpful throughout the whole thing. When administrators demonstrated levels of care and concern regarding Cameron in meetings and on evenings and weekends, we knew he was in a special place.

We had originally planned not to have a family vacation over the summer that year. We had gone to Disney World the previous six years, and it had been the highlight of Cameron's year each and every time. Seeing the characters he loved so much from movies always brought out the best in Cam. This year was different, however. Cameron didn't seem to be in a good state of mind, and we were concerned that such an overwhelming experience would be too taxing. After debating back and forth, we decided that not going and doing something he loved to do and was expecting to do might be a bad thing and send his spiral even further downward, so we decided to make the annual trek to Florida and try to cheer our boy up.

While we had glimmers of hope and happiness throughout the week in Florida, Cameron's underlying theme was high levels of tension and angst. He was missing the carefree and gleeful approach he had demonstrated in summers past. Although we couldn't put our fingers on why he was conflicted, it was painfully obvious that he was. The ease at which he worked himself up into a severe outburst was baffling. I cannot explain my feeling of shock at his sudden onset of physical aggressiveness toward Lisa, Mya, and me. Sure, I felt physical pain when being hit by a seventeen-year-old as anyone would expect, but it wasn't the physical side of things that hurt the most. It hurt my soul in way I'd never felt before.

The problem wasn't simply that our son was being physically aggressive toward us; it was that it varied so drastically from how we had grown to know Cameron. We could see the look of angst on his face throughout the day, and it hurt that we were unable to understand why he was feeling that way or communicate with him in ways he or we understood. Seeing him cry and be emotionally distraught after reaching the pinnacle of anger and striking out at us hurt. We had been on cruise control with Cameron for a long time, and suddenly we felt like we barely knew him.

Then came the start of the school year. We knew we were probably going to be in for a rough ride when we moved his planning board calendar in his room in August and began to write the key dates and activities. Writing the words "First day of school" was met by a firm and adamant "*NO* school" statement from Cameron. He meant it. Trying to get him to go to school the first day was met with severe outbursts, yelling unlike any we'd ever heard. He physically planted himself in an immovable way. It was clear he wasn't going to go. We needed to recalculate.

The school started midweek. We let the school know he wouldn't be there that week, but that we'd try again the following week. We had a conference call with the school that afternoon, and someone suggested bringing him in just to be in the school setting and see some of the changes they'd made, like the sensory hallway. Lisa and I reluctantly agreed to give that approach a try. He explored lightly but was ready to go home after about an hour, to which we obliged.

Cameron loves his iPhone and had pretty much unfettered access to it. Recall that while it offered him a source of entertainment, it offered us a glimpse into his world by way of search history. We thought maybe he believed that being at the house meant he would be able to play games or Google things on his phone all day, so we braced ourselves for the worst. We wrote a daily schedule for him that visually reinforced a new rule of school first, then phone. We removed all breakable items from within reach that Monday morning. When in a rage, he throws the nearest throwable object. We've replaced several light bulbs, headphones, candle holders, remote control devices, and so forth, but that morning everything was on lockdown. The result didn't get too bad. He showed more sadness than rage that morning, because he didn't want to leave. He cried a little when he said goodbye to Lisa, and I took him to school on my way to work. He had apparently developed severe separation anxiety that was adding to his tumultuous mindset and behavior.

We modified his start to the school year with some shorter days, to reduce the hours. All in all, the transition wasn't going too badly, he had moments of on-edge behavior. During that time, I got a call from Walmart headquarters regarding a position available in northwest Arkansas. It would be a chance to return home and put Cameron back in a place he was familiar with, perhaps an opportunity to restart the clock for him. After discussing the idea with Lisa, we decided to pursue the opportunity, not knowing what might come of it, but if it was meant to be, it was meant to be. I interviewed in mid-August for the position. Had we known for sure that it would either be a thumbs up or thumbs down, we would have reconsidered the school year for him, but with nothing for sure, we had to begin as if nothing was going to happen.

A Return Home

As it turns out, we had to make another transition, because I did end up getting offered and accepting the position. It may seem like the decision was simple, but I assure you it was anything but. We weighed this decision carefully; I enjoyed my role with Target and worked with an incredible team in the Midwest (go G194!). Moreover, the last thing we wanted to do was set Cameron back more than we felt had already occurred. That said, we had been given an opportunity to return home to a strong and solid network of friends and family. Back to a school and community Cameron was used to. Back to the running trails he talked about so often. Back to all the things familiar, and from what his Google search history showed, what was an ever-present topic on his mind. Ultimately, we determined that a chance to press Control/Alt/ Delete was the best decision we could make.

We decided to begin the process of informing Cam of the news. He was excited when we shared with him that it was going to be "Goodbye Olathe; hi, Bentonville" in early

September. He started naming off all the familiar destinations and activities of old–the Saturday long run, the Sunday trail run followed by donuts, plus Bentonville West High School and all his teachers there. Of all the things he demonstrated that day, though, we *loved* his expression when he saw the house we were moving into. While it wasn't the same house we had before when we were in Bentonville, it was similar. He let out an exuberant gasp when we saw the pictures. He was clearly happy to return.

All in all, things went smoothly. He had one small outburst at the end of the first week of school, but we believe it was primarily exploring boundaries, typical behavior of a boy. His friends at school were excited to see him as well. He grew up with most of the kids in his autism classroom. Their excitement as well as his when we walked in that first day was a welcome sight.

The first week of December 2019 will definitely be one that we will not forget - for several reasons. In many ways we had been on cruise control for several years in terms of life with autism. Granted, what we call normal is far from someone else's normal, but isn't that the same for every situation in life? It becomes easy to settle into a routine, and in large part we had, for the prior fourteen years. Sure, it was similar to a roller coaster with a lot of twists and turns, ups and downs with days and weeks not always looking the same and each having their own complexity, but year after year it's easy to get in a groove and handle your normal, whatever that normal is.

When Cameron turned eighteen in October 2019, it sparked the necessity to pursue guardianship of him. Until that point, he was our minor child, and there was no need to have any papers to speak on his behalf. That all changes when your minor child turns eighteen and the law says he's an adult. Suddenly Lisa and I found ourselves with a dependent adult. I chuckle a little when I say suddenly, because clearly we knew the day was coming for some time, but it's easy to bookmark that future chapter in your mind and keep it out there in the "someday" file that seems so far away. One day, though, you find yourself turning the page and facing that chapter.

I find it hard to explain the feeling I had of the guardianship process once Cameron turned eighteen. It is impossible to describe adequately, and more specifically describe the emotions that surround it. Two emotional moments stand out. The first was when Cameron had to be served papers letting him know someone was pursuing guardianship of him. The process was required by state law, and obviously for good reason. While hard to believe, some people actually take advantage of other people, and the process of serving papers guards against that possibility.

The person serving the papers called us the day prior, to set a time. When he came inside the house, we got Cameron and introduced him to the man. As the process demands, the server read the required paperwork to Cameron.

I don't know why, but I felt a huge rush of emotion that I cannot explain. I watched Cameron oblivious to what was happening, looking at the guy but probably what is better described as looking through the guy. I knew Cameron didn't understand the process; I knew it because Cameron's cognitive limitations are not something we were ever naïve about. Maybe it was something about Cameron having to be in a situation he didn't understand and the innocence in his eyes, the childlike laughter from him as he repeated a few of his favorite SpongeBob phrases. Whatever it was, I felt a wide range of emotion when the event took place as did Lisa.

The second event for us was the actual court date itself. Cam would need to be with us as part of the process. We met our attorney about a half hour before court began, and he let us know what we should expect. He told us that when the guardianship case was announced we would go up near the judge's bench. Our attorney said he (our attorney) would ask us about a dozen qualifying questions that we would affirm, and then the judge would ask some questions. He mentioned that this particular judge was one who asks several questions and told us to just answer them to the best of our ability and address the judge. All in all, it would take about ten to fifteen minutes.

We settled into the courtroom after a few minutes of Cameron doing some of his OCD tics. He had recently picked up the necessity of taking a 360-degree turn around and do-ing three jumps with both feet before tiptoe-walking to the destination. Similar to all OCD behavior, it was something that Cameron had to do to make a transition, and no one was going to convince him otherwise, regardless the setting. In the house, it was one thing. Even in most public settings it was something that happened quickly and was over. In a courtroom setting, though, it seemed like that fifteen seconds of transition lasted twenty minutes. We were sitting near the front of the public seating section of the courtroom.

A few divorce cases were in front of our case, which, let me say, was odd to sit through, as I thought how public a dis-play it was for people going through a very private situation.

That's apparently the process, however, and our guardianship would be no different. The judge then called the guardianship case of Cameron Leachman to the floor.

I thought the transition into the courtroom felt like it took forever, but when our name was called the transition from where we were sitting to get in front of the judge felt like a lifetime. Cam had to do his obligatory 360-degree spins and jumps, except that time we got held up slightly by the waist-high swinging doors from the public-seating section into the official area of the courtroom where we interacted with the judge. The slight delay prompted the necessity to restart the 360-degree turn plus three-jump process before finally sitting down in the rolling chair. The transition into the rolling chair posed some additional challenges for Cam, as he was only used to sitting down on stationary chairs he could lean back into on his way down. It took a couple of attempts, and some assisting and prompting from Lisa and me, but we finally got him settled.

The interaction with the judge started, except it didn't. When Cameron got settled, we looked up at the judge, and he simply said, "I am going to grant you guardianship of your son." He had a caring and compassionate look on his face that I do not think I will ever forget. He had some follow up statements explaining the process to us, the requirement to file an annual report with the court regarding Cameron's circumstances, and such, the warning that if we missed that process within a sixty-day window we would be arrested, but we were dismissed almost as soon as we were seated. The event was surreal, and our attorney stated as much when we reconvened outside the courtroom. He said he had never experienced that judge not asking any questions.

That entire morning was an emotional roller coaster for me, similar to the feelings evoked in me when Cam was being served the notice of hearing. There were emotions felt that are impossible to explain as I watched him in such a big setting unaware of the situation and the social norms of behavior in a courtroom. It moved me to watch everyone who interacted with him that morning—our attorney, people in the courtroom, the bailiff—do so with such care. Lastly, the compassionate interaction with the judge and hearing the words "incapacitated person" out loud for the first time in Cameron's life was an unexpectedly emotional experience for both Lisa and me.

We transitioned from the courthouse to the Department of Motor Vehicles to get Cameron a state ID, one of those other things we had been trying to avoid because of the setting. Sitting and waiting was tough enough for Cam, but he has always had an aversion to children crying, sometimes escalating to the desire to hit the child on the head, which we have had to deal with a few times throughout Cameron's life – from young child to late teens. Anyone who has had the pleasure of sitting in the DMV for any length of time knows it's not only going to be a wait, but you are likely going to interact with a crying child. The environment of boredom brings out the best in all of us, adults and children alike.

I don't know if there is ever a good time to visit the DMV, but luck was on our side that day. Only a handful of people waited in front of us in the ID line, and Cameron seemed more tolerant of the environment that day. We had a twenty-minute wait or so, and only a couple of young children were crying, but Cameron kept his headphones on and only stared at the crying children with curiosity.

At one point he yelled, "What's your name?", a warning sign of potential escalation, to one of the kids, because he wanted to engage with him from a distance, but thankfully the situation de-escalated quickly, and we were soon at the front of the line. He did well with the ID process and having his picture taken. Again, everyone we encountered that day was cool with Cameron. The parent of a special-needs child can have no greater feeling than being in a setting where the child is not being "normal," whatever that is, and yet all others are accommodating and understanding.

Getting the guardianship and state IDs were big moments for us, but it was on the drive home that we received news that was completely unexpected. It was the results of some bloodwork for Cam taken earlier in the week. About ten days prior he had experienced some significant foot swelling that was unexplained. Granted, for the previous seven or eight months Cameron had developed an avoidance behavior of sitting down in any environment he was in. His default, unless absolutely necessary, such as a car ride, was to stand, so he would. He'd stand all day long. In large part we felt like part of the issue with swelling was gravity induced and a symptom of standing, albeit we had not noted any swelling in the previous several months, despite his having the same behavior.

During the time when he stopped sitting, Cameron was still running with me. He had slowed quite a bit, but all of his motions were the same, without obvious signs of pain. We had x-rays and PT evaluations done to rule out anything glaring that we might be missing. Neither revealed any issues. His Google history, where we would normally see he had searched for pain terms if he was hurting, was devoid of any searching for knee, foot, or back pain. We chalked the constant standing and intense OCD up to a sensory tic, something we have seen come and go and something we would continue to work with the school to implement trial and error solutions in both environments until we found what worked.

When the foot swelling started, it kicked the "something is definitely not right" side of my brain into high gear. Now, I don't often consult Facebook for serious issues, because opinions run rampant on there, but some good things do sometimes come out of it, so while we waited for Cam's doctor to get back from vacation, I consulted the great Doctor Facebook. I received a lot of opinions, but through the comments, instant messages, text messages, and phone calls I received after posting, one theme was clear: we should do some testing for underlying issues.

Having a doctor who will collaborate with you is *vital* throughout any journey with autism, so we are deeply thankful for ours. Being willing to sit down and explore options and discuss pros and cons and different approaches is a priceless characteristic. We ultimately decided on doing several panels for just about everything one can test with bloodwork. That process brought about a whole new set of anxiety and nerves in me. Cam had never had blood drawn–at least not once he was old enough to understand. He is also a man-child who was strong and unpredictable in situations he doesn't want to be in. Our biggest fear was that he would do something when that needle was stuck in his arm. Our worries were quickly set by the wayside when we went in the room. The nurses at the Children's Hospital were good with him, putting him at ease. I helped secure his free hand to avoid any adverse or sudden reaction. Almost as quickly as it started, it was over. We were soon on our way to check out and let him pick up his sticker. He chose Buzz Lightyear that day.

Cameron's doctor called the morning of our court appointment just as we entered the building and were seated in the area right outside the courtroom. She left a message that she had received Cam's blood test results and to call her when we got the chance. I sent her a text message letting her know we had just gotten into the courtroom and it might be forty-five minutes or so before I had a chance to call, to which she replied that was fine, just give her a call whenever.

I am sure I am not in the minority here when I say the *absence* of the words "everything came back normal" struck instant concern in me. It wasn't in the text or in the voicemail. My only experience to compare it to was my own doctor appointments where the doctor called and left detailed messages as to results from any lab work if I wasn't able to pick up. Both Lisa and I wondered if something could be wrong, and we discussed the possibility quietly. We rationalized it was just a matter of practice for her not to give results by text or voicemail. Yes, that must be it.

As soon as we exited the courtroom that day we called her. Most of the results came back normal. The exception was the test measuring the ASO, a measure of the antibodies produced by the body in response to a strep infection – different than simply having strep throat.

Here's where I need to insert a disclaimer. I don't profess to be a medical professional; I am relaying this information in a simplified form.

Cameron's levels of ASO were nearly four times the

normal results for an adult. While it was likely the cause of the swelling, we learned more in our discussion with the doctor that day. Apparently, the elevated levels of ASO can create a condition known as PANDAS, short for Pediatric Autoimmune Neuropsychiatric Disorders Associated with Streptococcal Infections. Children with PANDAS may exhibit OCD, tic disorder, or both, either suddenly or worse than usual. Many of the symptoms that had so sporadically started with Cameron some fourteen to eighteen months earlier, including the intense and rapid onset of OCD, aggressive behavior, and the lack of desire and willingness to sit, could be linked to PANDAS. The standard treatment is a three-month course of antibiotics, but despite everything we read, we should see noticeable changes within the first week or so.

Let me tell you, we were shocked with what we saw in very short order of Cameron starting the antibiotics. Within three days we saw significant changes in both swelling and behavior. I'll never forget that Sunday morning after he started the antibiotics on Thursday. He *sat* at the kitchen table with me for about three hours! I was doing some work, but I had given him the advertisements from the Sunday paper, full of Christmas toys, because Christmas was only a few weeks away. He sat and flipped through the paper or played with his phone the entire time, something that would have previously been only a ten-to-fifteen-minute occurrence, if at all. Later that afternoon I found him lying on his bed playing with some toys, something he used to do, but we had not seen him do it for well over seven months. Both Lisa and I were so happy to see Cameron returning to the kiddo (though now an adult) we had known for so long. I took several pictures that day and shared them with his teacher, our family, and others. While it was a big day, we also felt horrible for not considering his behavioral changes might have been the result of an illness—a curable one—before. Back when Cameron started having behavior issues and severe OCD, we immediately chalked it up to behavior intervention.

In the short span of a few days on his antibiotic he showed marked improvement in nearly every part of his life. All swelling was gone, and the sitting, lying on bed, and walking normally have all continued or gotten better. I have seen a *huge* difference in the approach he has to his runs. Soon he had an overt desire to run, and his happiness during our runs reminded me of how he was a little more a year earlier.

In hindsight I wish we had stepped back and evaluated the situation to explore and rule out any underlying medical issue. The incident goes back to something I brought up earlier: don't stop having conversations with your doctor and keep a journal. Even as an "autism veteran," we had miscalculated and jumped to conclusions without exploring.

Phases and Lessons–The Autism Journey

Life with Cameron is both routine and sporadically new at the same time. What is interesting is how many different phases Cameron has gone through that are difficult in the moment and seem to last forever, but eventually fade naturally or with intervention. A few of that come top of mind include the following:

The non-potty-trained phase. I'll be honest, we didn't think this phase would ever subside. Cameron was still in diapers through the age of nine. While there is nothing fun about changing a diaper on a child of any age, changing a nine-year-old is a challenge. We are thankful for the strategies his elementary teacher suggested that helped get us through that phase. He first started using the bathroom in school but wanted to rely on diapers at home. This experience taught us the importance of simulating the school environment at home as well. The two should not have competing expectations, as it creates confusion for the child. We have stuck to the on-the-same-page approach for many things throughout

Cameron's life, where we strived to be in lockstep with the school to keep things consistent for Cam. When we bought our last package of diapers and moved Cameron to big-boy underwear, we thought it worthy of throwing a celebration, though we didn't do it.

Sticking to the theme of bodily functions, one of the other phases Cameron went through in his mid-teen years was the unwillingness and lack of desire to wipe his bottom. One would think this behavior would have presented itself during the potty-training timeframe or shortly after; however, it was a phase he went through late in his junior high days. It started completely out of the blue one day when he had used the bathroom and summoned Lisa and me to the restroom. When he first said, "This one" as he pointed to the toilet paper, we thought he wanted reassurance that we wanted him to wipe. It was soon obvious that what he had zero desire to do so and was not budging. I know it sounds easy to apply simple logic to the situation and just not budge as a parent, but any parent of a special-needs child will tell you that sometimes, actually very often, the will of the child is ironclad. It was clear to us that we could either assist in the moment or have a virtual real mess on our hands if he got up. Thankfully his bowel movements occurred before or after school, so the school staff didn't have to deal with the situation.

For a few months we fought his refusal to wipe himself and allowed ourselves to be summoned to the restroom when needed. We were clueless as to what prompted the change and more importantly unenlightened on how to stop it. Our constant reminder to ourselves and to each other was that it could be worse; at least he was using the restroom, and the regression and new habit included only not wiping. One day Lisa's mom suggested we try latex gloves with Cameron, that maybe gloves would give him a sense of protection for his hands. It worked!! He put on a pair of gloves when he used the restroom and then required no assistance. We had to remain diligent in checking the restroom afterwards, however, as his default behavior was to drop the gloves anywhere other than in the trash can located conveniently next to the toilet. One day, nearly a year after the behavior started out of the blue, we noticed Cameron stopped using the gloves and had resumed normal bathroom behavior.

Around the same time of the random stoppage of wiping his hiney, Cameron also started excessive handwashing throughout the day. This cycle was one that had no impact on us, but it was heartbreaking to watch. It was also one of the longest running cycles we had encountered with Cam, lasting just shy of two years. During this time Cameron started demonstrating some OCD tics, with handwashing seemingly tied to it. He washed his hands upwards of thirty times a day, often back to back, where he would dry his hands and then restart the process. And when I say handwashing, I mean intense handwashing–long lasting. At its peak we struggled to fight the sores on his hands from the excessive washing. To help offset the sores we sneaked in his room when he was sleeping and put lotion on his hands. Cameron did not like lotion at all and putting it on during the day would only prompt another handwashing session. Thankfully we were able to work with Cam to reduce the frequency of the handwashing, focusing first on duration and reducing the time for each wash and finally reducing the number of times he engaged in the activity.

When Cameron was in high school, we were finally able to transition him to showering independently. This challenge had been one of the longer lasting ones, that seems much more of a "will" thing rather than a "skill" thing that went back to the willpower I mentioned earlier. Through the time Cam started junior high, he had a lack of desire to engage in any sort of helpful behavior during showers, relying heavily on Lisa or me to assist. Slowly we were able to transition him to perform the tasks himself, though intent and effectiveness are two very different things. Each action required prompting, as in "wash your arms" or "wash your legs." Cameron's version of washing any body part was simply one part of the wash scrunchie touching it or one swipe across one part of it. That said, showering still needed a high level of intervention to make sure he maintained good hygiene. Persistence is everything with Cameron, and eventually we were able to help him grasp the concept of washing himself appropriately. As it stands today, Cam performs all the actions, with heavy prompting by us. Taking incremental steps toward independent task completion is the key to success.

Cam has gone through a few "Eeww, that's gross" phases as well. He went through a finger-licking phase in elementary school that lasted about five months. When I say finger-licking, I am not referencing something moderate, such as after eating food. I am talking about sticking each finger on both hands completely in his mouth repetitively throughout the day. Obviously, we had concerns of what he was exposing himself to, aside from the calluses he was creating on his fingers.

There was the "Photo of my food" phase that Cameron went through during the same time he started cooking with Lisa. He would borrow her phone to take pictures of ingredients and of the plated food. It was customary before every meal for Cameron to ask, "Picture?" which he followed by taking a picture of his plate. When I say he took a picture of every meal, I mean it literally. It didn't matter whether it was at home or out to eat, if it was a meal, he took a picture of it. We kept a separate folder on the phone because he liked to go through it a lot. He was spot on with his photography skills. Those pics were on point!

Cameron went through about a year-long stretch in late junior high and high school of taking his chewed food out of his mouth during any meal. He started by sticking his tongue out with food on it and attempting to look at it and then changed into actually taking a handful out to evaluate, and then he stuck it back in his mouth. There's no telling the goal of this activity, but we were happy to see it subside after we worked with him on socially acceptable behavior.

When Cameron was eighteen, he went through one of his shortest-lived and most perplexing phases. He started touching his eyeball before he transitioned to a new task. He did it to the point of creating extremely red and irritated eyes. We knew we needed to get him away from that behavior quickly. History had proven that once he started something it was prone to become a hard-wired activity that remained for some time, and there is nothing healthy about touching one's eyeball. Thankfully Lisa had the idea of having him tapping his nose two times instead of touching his eyeball, and it worked! He gladly traded in an eyeball-touch for two nose-taps.

The "horsey" phase is one that recently started. This is where Cameron wants a horsey ride (piggyback) to bed each night. The hardest time with this phase was hauling him up a flight of stairs in our Kansas home. Trust me when I say I wish he hadn't started this phase when he was nearly six feet tall and 160 pounds, but it's hard to refuse any time he wants to engage with me. I assume the role of Bullseye, the horse from *Toy Story*, each night around 9:30 and await him to finish brushing his teeth so he can run gleefully to the living room and jump on my back. If you have never experienced the joy of 160 pounds jumping on your back, I highly recommend it. ☺ That said, I wouldn't change it for the world!

We also endured the "teeth hard" and "puppy dog" phases. I know, I know, these phases have some interesting names, but Cam himself named them. He comes up with his interpretation and name for every activity. At some point in middle school he became fascinated with people's mouths—more specifically Lisa's and mine.

He'd get a kick out of asking Lisa for "teeth hard," which was his way of telling her to put her teeth together and kind of smile. Basically, if you can imagine putting your teeth together and opening your lips to expose the teeth, that was it. He just stares curiously for ten or fifteen seconds while tapping her cheeks with his hand, and then it is over.

The "Puppy dog, please, Dad" activity is pretty much him wanting me to pant like a puppy with my mouth as wide as possible, so he can investigate. Sometimes it's followed with the statement "tongue," which is when he wants me to stick my tongue out like a dog would after running.

Yes, both these activities seem crazy, and it never matters to Cameron whether we are in a public place, driving, or home. There is no rhyme or reason for when he asks for it, but we almost always accommodate him. I know it seems awkward for those around us when it happens in a public place, and we debate our internal battle of whether to engage or teach a lesson on socially acceptable behavior whenever it happens in public. But let me let you in on a little secret. Parents of special-needs kids, particularly more severely delayed kids like Cam, don't get to interact with their kids in the same way a typical parent would. Each and every interaction where they invite you into their world, especially the unprompted ones, is precious. Judge if you must, but I will shamelessly assume the role of a puppy dog anytime and all the time.

Then there's what I call the "Old MacDonald" phase that is still very much active today. We recently discovered Cameron loves cows and roosters, which we had no clue about until our recent move. The where area we live is on the outskirts of Bentonville, the result of which is some real rural route options for our morning run. The joy on this kid's face when he sees the rooster he hears crowing is wonderful to see. It's the same emotion he demonstrates when the cows are next to the fence line. He wants to stop and talk to the rooster or the cows anytime we run by them. Hearing him mimic either is pretty cool.

One of Cam's favorite running routes

One morning we were out for a run and the farmer was driving by. I flagged him down and introduced Cam to him. It doesn't take folks long to figure out something is unique about Cam, and this interaction was no exception. I worried that it would look like we were messing with the cows and wanted the farmer to know why we stopped that day. I knew from past examples that it wouldn't be the last time we stopped. I mentioned to the farmer that we weren't bothering the cows; it was just something Cameron seemed to be into, and it was a side of Cameron I'd never seen before. The farmer invited us to the dairy farm to let Cameron feed the calves. You talk about excited! Watching Cameron's gleeful face as he got to bottle feed a calf for the first time is too hard to describe, but it was really cool.

We have discovered one of my favorite parts of Cameron's farm-animal affinity on our Sunday afternoon drives. Every Sunday at 1:30 we go for a drive out in the country. When we get to an intersection, I let him tell me which way to turn. His strong preference is dirt roads. We always stop when we come across livestock, be it alpacas, cows, donkeys, horses, roosters, or sheep. Cameron will stare and talk to them, imitating their sounds, until I finally drive on. He'd ride forever if we could, but eventually I have to get us back home. Cameron's fascination with farm animals has made Lisa and me want to find some type of country home where we can have some farm animals for his future.

My all-time favorite phase Cameron went through was what I affectionately call the "Cameron Laugh" phase. One thing has been constant with Cam throughout his life; if he likes something it will become hard programmed into his brain as routine from the first time he experiences it. Such was the case with "Cameron Laugh." It started one evening when he was in middle school, about the time we started running and our bond was strengthening. I was taking something to his room and he asked, "Puppy dog please, Dad." While in the middle of embracing my innermost pup, I tickled his side, which is *super* ticklish, I discovered. I pinned him down and tickled his head, which seemed somewhat therapeutic to him. Every so often I raised my hands high in the air and brought them crashing down to start tickling his sides again. He tried to buck me off, and then we'd repeat. Very similar to the way we started running, I didn't know this routine was going to be a standard at seven o'clock nightly until the following night, when he came and found me and said, "Cameron laugh." I wasn't quite sure what he meant, but figured it out quickly when he put my hands on his head. It became a nightly routine, though he just recently stopped asking for it every night, and it seems to be more sporadic of late.

We are currently going through a "hop three times and toe walk" phase. Every transition, be it from one room to the other, one task to another, or from house to car, is preempted by a series of three hops along with tiptoeing. Something sensory seeking is about it that we will eventually figure out. We know it is sensory seeking/avoiding because if it doesn't feel just right, he will start the sequence over again. We've tried a small trampoline in his room, hoping he would fulfill the input need by jumping on something more appropriate and, might I add, better for his feet. My biggest fear with this phase is when he does it on the hardwood or tile floors with bare feet in the morning or evening. I worry he might injure his foot in some way. He has reduced this behavior of late, which gives me hope we are nearing the end of this phase. Fingers crossed this one will pass quickly!

Along with the many phases Cam has gone through, we as parents go through a recurring phase as well. I'd be remiss if I didn't bring it up. Transparently, Lisa and I go through our fair share of "being human." There is a hidden challenge of raising a high-need child that someone who hasn't experienced could never understand. It is something especially difficult when coupled with severe behavior issues like Cameron was exhibiting throughout much of his teen years. It's the strain on a relationship between husband and wife. It's real. To talk about it out loud always, and I mean always, feels like you blame your child, and for that reason neither Lisa nor I say much about it outside of conversations with each other. I think much has to do with the desire to protect the world's view of Cameron. The last thing either of us want is for someone to look at Cam as a burden to us. We don't feel that way.

That said, do we feel a bit of envy at the spontaneity with which others get to approach life? Yes, without doubt. The feeling comes up occasionally. We'd love to be able to do things on a whim. We'd love to be able to live as carefree in life as other parents with two young adults. We'd be lying if we said throughout Cameron's life we didn't look at other parents and their ability to go to festivals, parades, or any number of other events as a family and wish we had the same capability. The reality of life with a special needs child is that your life looks totally different from others, and it can place a strain on a relationship. To bring this subject full circle, we continuously remind ourselves of the saying I referenced in the foreword, "Someone out there would love to live the life you have."

Lisa and I have gone through our hard times. Heck, we still have moments today. At one point during Cameron's severe behavior issues we couldn't trust him with anyone and didn't have a date night for nearly two years. During that time, we canceled a couple of trips we had planned to "escape" for a few days—one to Colorado and the other to Florida. There was just way too much risk that Cameron might have a severe meltdown and cause someone harm, so we could not be away, either locally or out of state.

I would like to share two more things with all parents of a special-needs child going through challenges today: stick it out together and don't compare your life to others.

No doubt your life will look very different from many of those in your social circle; however, comparing your life to someone else's is a recipe for disaster. One saying I love is "Comparison is the thief of joy." It's a fact. The minute you let yourself dwell on what you don't have or what you can't do, it starts you on a slippery slope downward. Grab your life by the horns and live the heck out of it.

Life with Cameron has certainly taught me a lot. I thought it would be fun to sum up the biggest lessons in life thus far.

Find a doctor who cares.

You owe it to yourself and your child to find a doctor who cares. I cannot understate this point. When you have a doctor who cares and who will take the time to truly understand your concerns and discuss (key word here) potential strategies for what you are going through, it makes a world of difference.

We didn't discover such a doctor until later in Cam's life, but we are thankful we found someone who cares.

You can be early, but never late.

Cameron has taught me the importance of punctuality. There is no such thing as being fashionably late with autism. If you commit to something happening at seven o'clock, 6:50 is okay, but 7:00:01 creates a lot of anxiety. It's funny how hard-coded punctuality becomes in one's way of life. When we have things we are invited to, we always arrive early. When we invite people over, we start looking at our watches at 1 minute past the time they are supposed to be there.

Life isn't about you.

I took the selfish route for far too long. Life quickly needs to become being about those in your life with the highest need. Every decision we make in our family is run through the filter of "How will this impact Cameron?"

Be relentless.

No one will be a bigger champion for you or your child than you. While you will have support networks in place, don't ever forget that you are your child's biggest advocate. Challenge the status quo and don't always accept a first proposed approach. There is absolutely nothing wrong with asking for proof that something is working. Don't feel bad for holding people/organizations accountable to their commitments when it comes to your child.

The squeaky wheel gets the grease.

You have to be a relentless advocate for your child. When you are in a system, remember that you are one of many and your voice should be the one heard most often.

No one knows your child better than you.

While we always lean on professional advice and input, we are also keenly aware that we know Cameron better than anyone else who isn't around him as much as we are.

Trust your gut in moments when your input is needed, and don't back down. IEP meetings with the school are good examples of times you need to stand your ground when you feel passionately about something. It can be intimidating and sometimes overwhelming to sit in a room of professionals. It's easy to disqualify your own opinion sometimes, but don't! If you find those settings challenging to tackle, I highly recommend finding an advocate to take with you. That's your right.

You have a voice, don't be afraid to use it.

Whether you are with your doctor, the school, or the public, you have to be vocal. Depending on your child's capabilities, you may be their only voice. Cameron has a limited vocabulary, and I am undoubtedly his voice quite often.

Plug into the world around you.

Parents helping parents is a beautiful thing, and multiple options are available locally or in the social media world. For much of Cameron's early days we didn't have things like Facebook groups to plug into. A word of caution on this, though: opinions run rampant, and filtering the input on social media pages is important. The information can be overwhelming at times and at times may be incorrect.

Not everyone is out to get you; many are there to help.

This kind of ties into the reference above about tempering involvement and advice from social media groups. There are a lot of opinions out there – especially about schools – and forming your own opinion is important. We have always found it effective to take an approach of strong partnership, consistent communication and proactive planning. In our situation, the majority of people we have interacted with in Cameron's school setting were fans of him and desired only the best for him.

People can be absolutely insensitive, rude, and cruel.

Sometimes out of ignorance, sometimes out of stupidity, people can be insensitive, rude, and cruel. All people deserve to be informed. I have zero issues with addressing someone who has disgustingly used the word *retarded* in an inappropriate way. Never apologize for being an advocate for your child.

Focusing on limits results in limits.

I fell into the trap of focusing on Cameron's limits for much of his early life. The lens through which I looked at him was focused exclusively on Cameron's limits. We have had some wonderful and revealing experiences when I tried something new with the thought that Cameron *could* do it.

Don't ever stop searching for a way to connect.

It took years for Cameron and me to find our groove and bond, but we are inseparable best friends now. I wouldn't define the searching I did with Cameron as intentional. Nearly all the connections we have forged have been organic and random. But the path to our connection is rooted in having an approach of not giving up and not focusing on limits

Raising a child and now having an adult with autism isn't without challenges, but I wouldn't trade it for the world. Cameron and I are best friends now with an inseparable bond. It didn't happen overnight, however. The recipe for our current state was twofold. First and foremost, my wife never gave up on me, despite having every possible valid reason to do so. Second, I had to be okay with me. Improving myself had a lot, if not everything to do with improving my situation. It reminds me of those pre-flight warnings to place the oxygen mask on you before helping those around you. You can't expect to be able to have a meaningful relationship with those around you if you don't believe in yourself first.

It's been a roller coaster for sure. Life with Cameron has had its ups and downs, twists and turns. It's had moments of fear and moments of jubilation. And similar a ride on a roller coaster, there is no possible way to explain it to someone who hasn't experienced it. Looking back on our life now, I am thankful I didn't give up when every part of me wanted to. I'd be missing out on a close relationship with one of the coolest dudes I know—my son.

If I could leave you with one thing it would be this: don't ever give up. Your best days are right around the corner.

#bestfriends

CPSIA information can be obtained
at www.ICGtesting.com
Printed in the USA
BVHW030216110320
574716BV00001B/95